FOR ORGANS, PIANOS & ELECTRONIC KEYBOARDS

E-Z PLAY TODAY

86

LEONARD COHEN

ISBN 978-1-5400-2230-1

HAL•LEONARD®

7777 W. BLUEMOUND RD. P.O. BOX 13819 MILWAUKEE, WI 53213

In Australia Contact:
Hal Leonard Australia Pty. Ltd.
4 Lentara Court
Cheltenham, Victoria, 3192 Australia
Email: ausadmin@halleonard.com.au

Visit Hal Leonard Online at
www.halleonard.com

Anthem

Registration 3
Rhythm: Slow Rock or 6/8 March

Words and Music by
Leonard Cohen

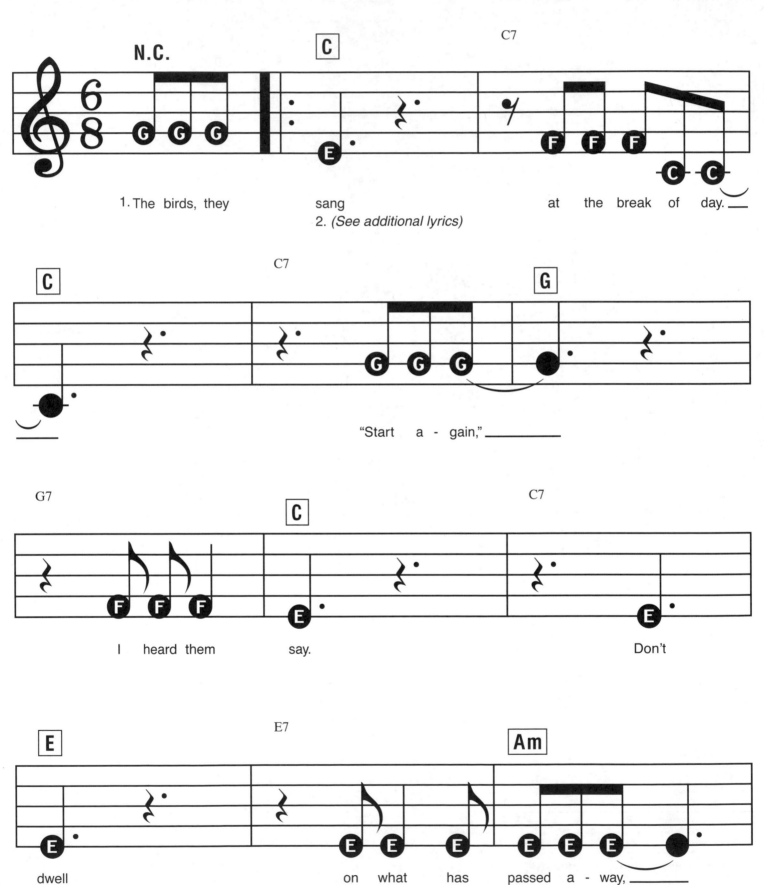

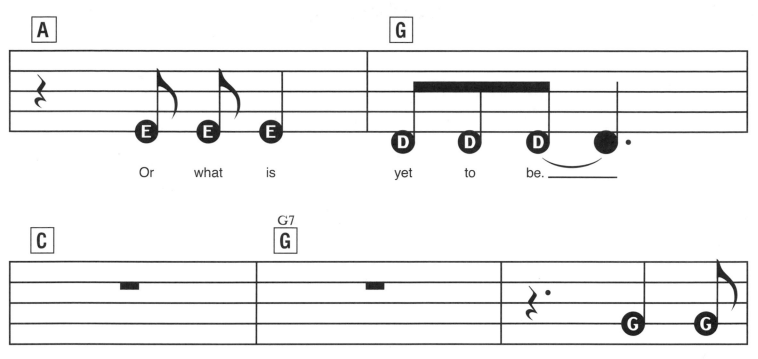

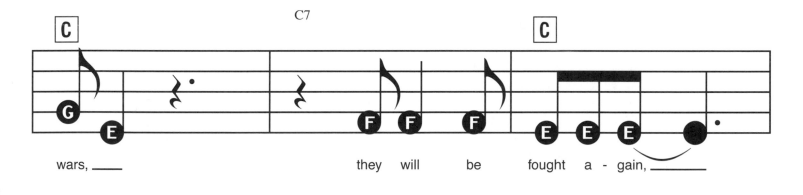

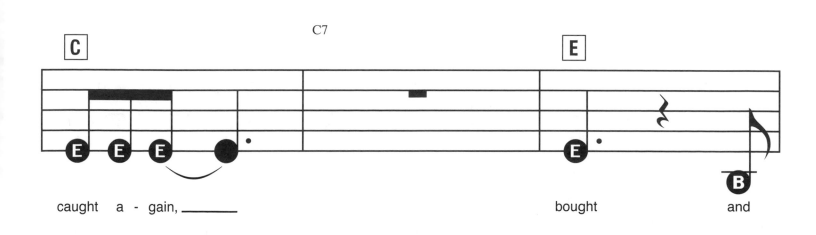

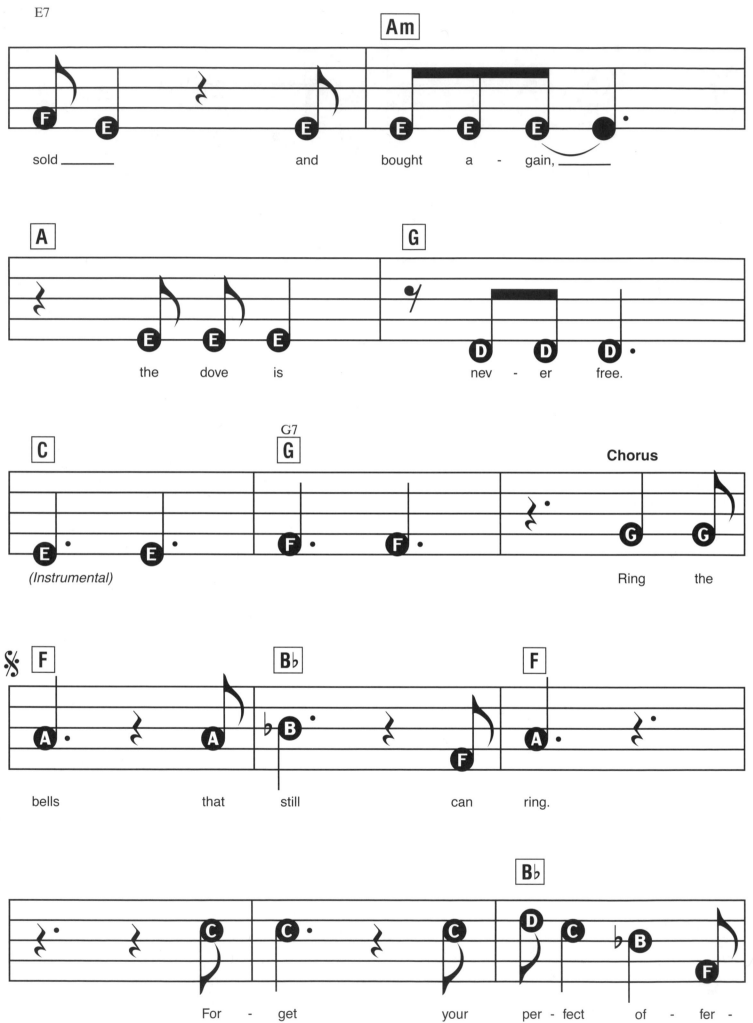

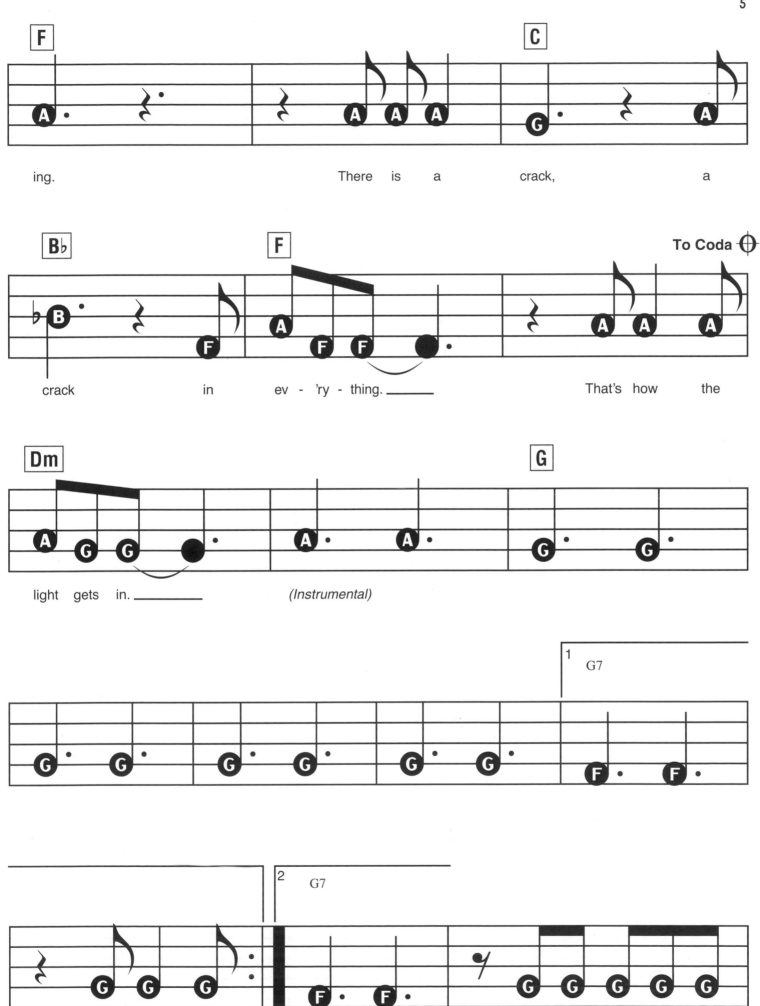

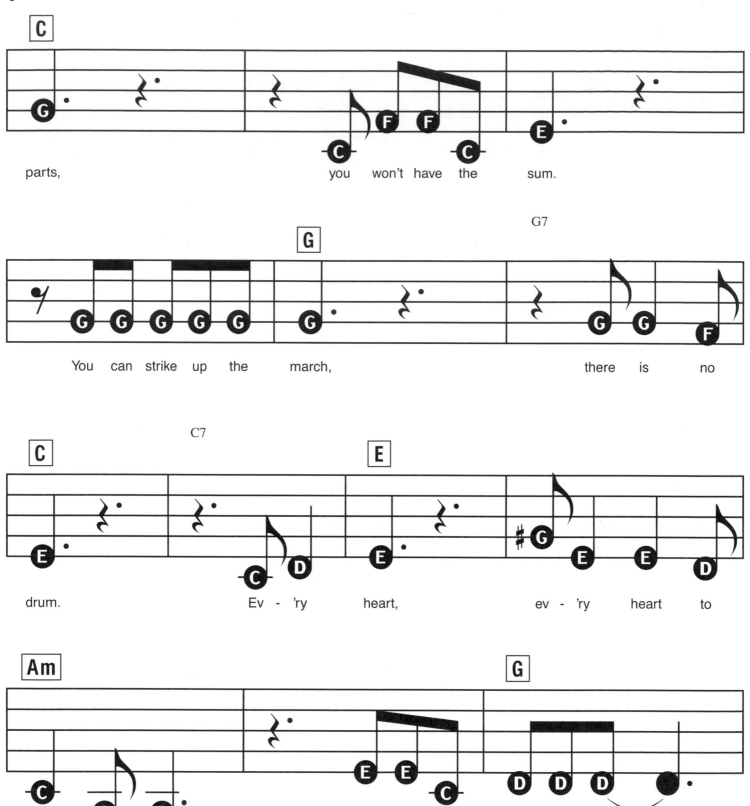

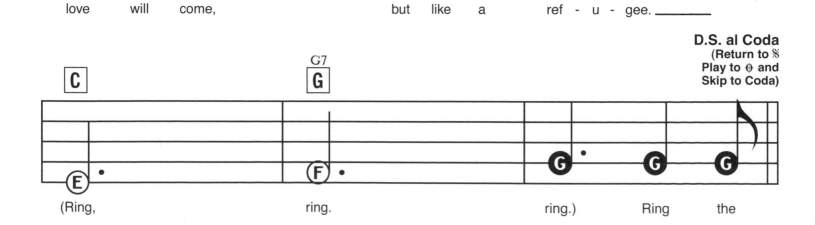

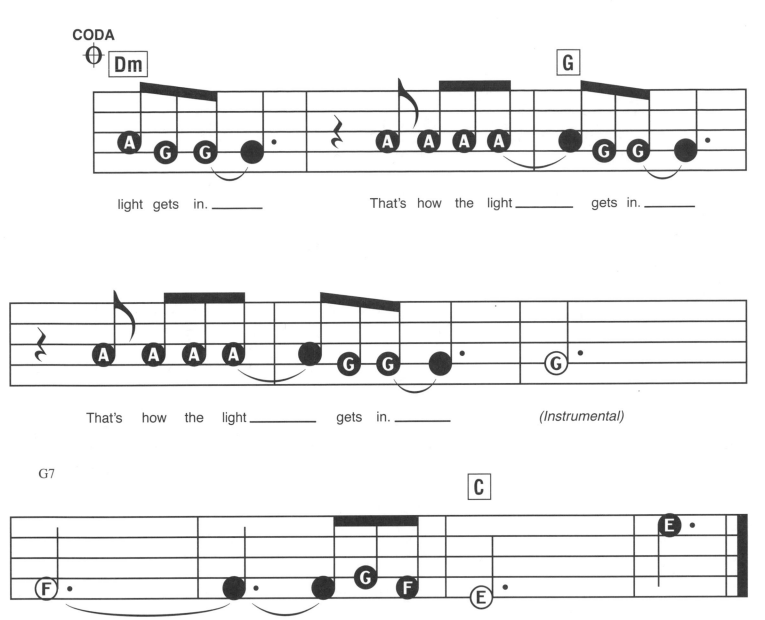

CODA

light gets in. _____ That's how the light _____ gets in. _____

That's how the light _____ gets in. _____ *(Instrumental)*

Additional Lyrics

2. We asked for signs, the signs were sent,
   The birth betrayed, the marriage spent.
   Yeah, the widowhood of every government,
   Signs for all to see.

   I can't run no more with that lawless crowd
   While the killers in high places say their prayers out loud.
   But they've summoned up a thundercloud,
   They're going to hear from me.

Bird on the Wire
(Bird on a Wire)

Registration 4
Rhythm: Waltz

Words and Music by
Leonard Cohen

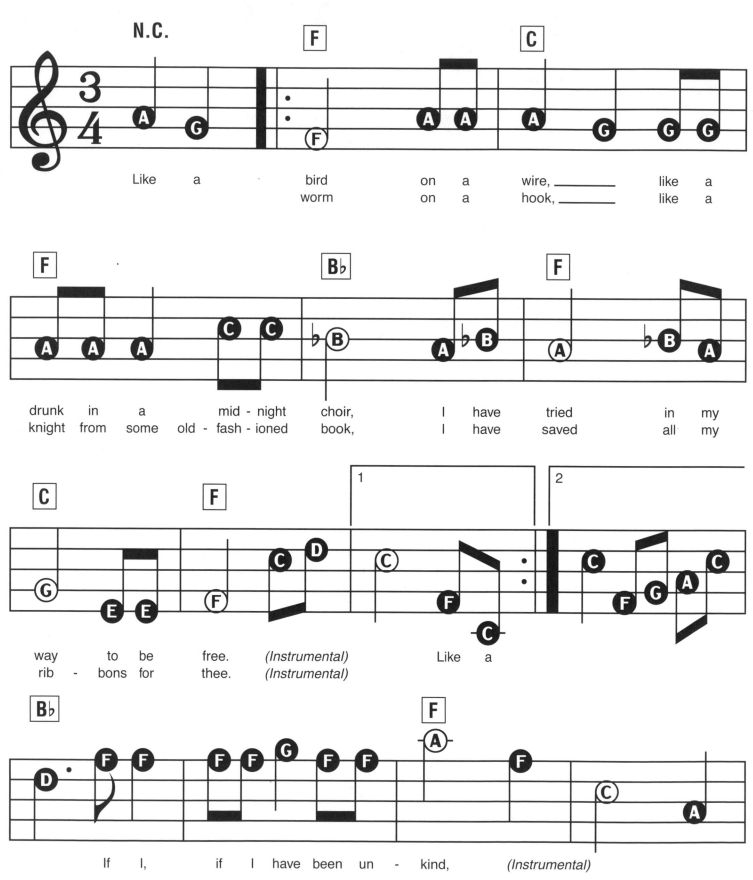

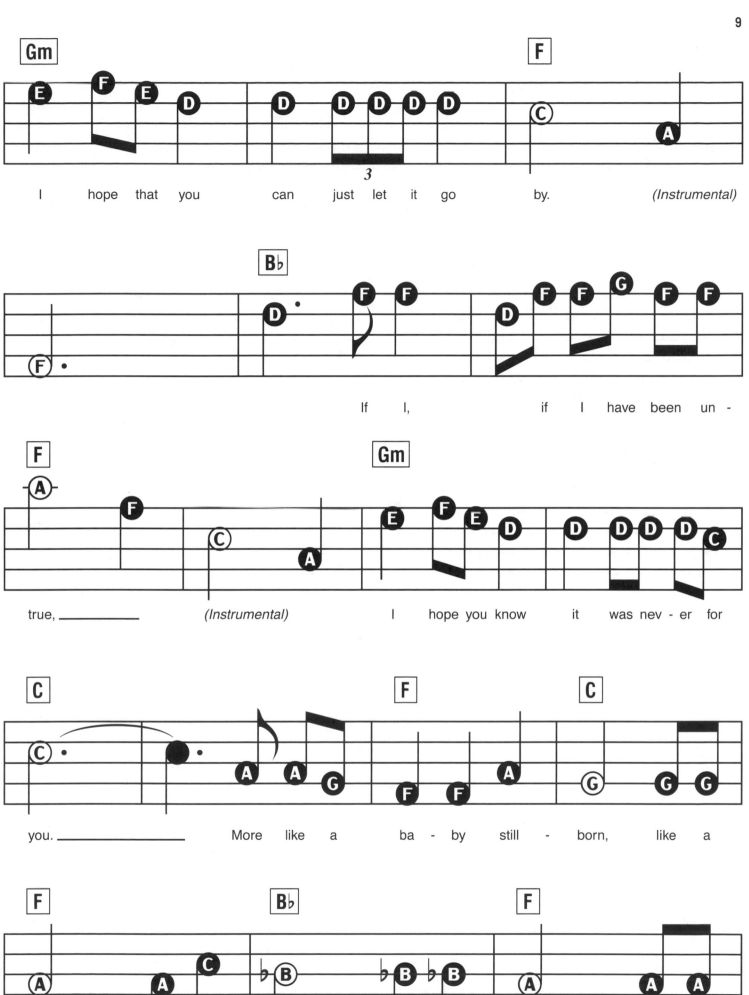

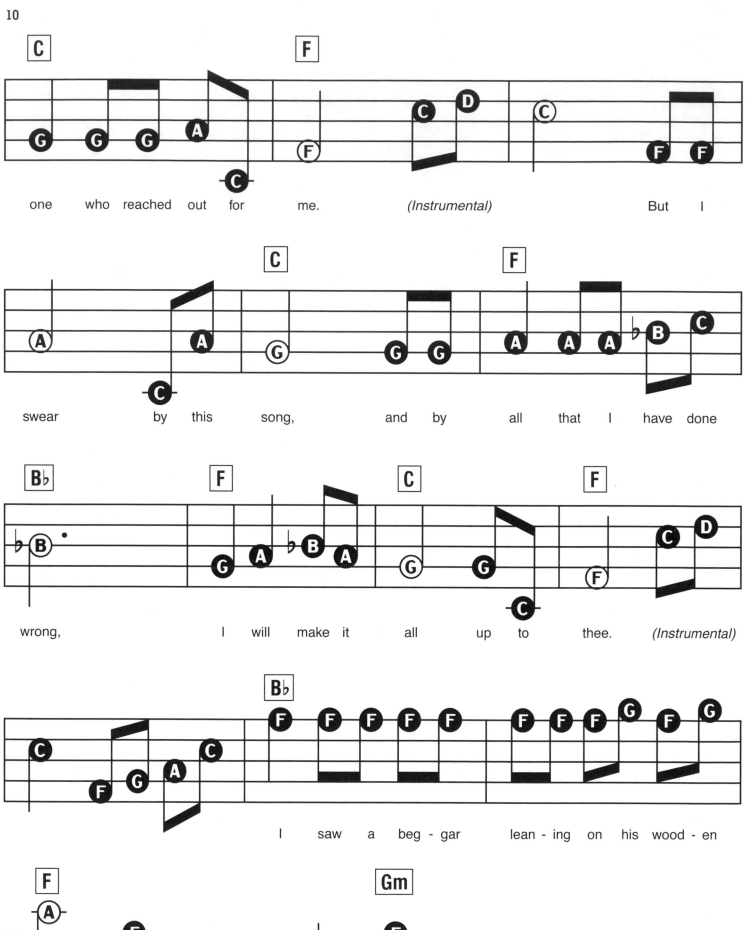
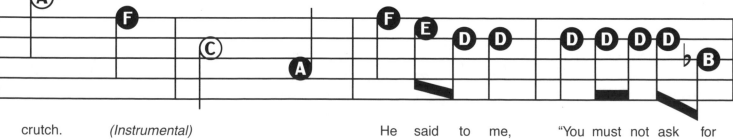

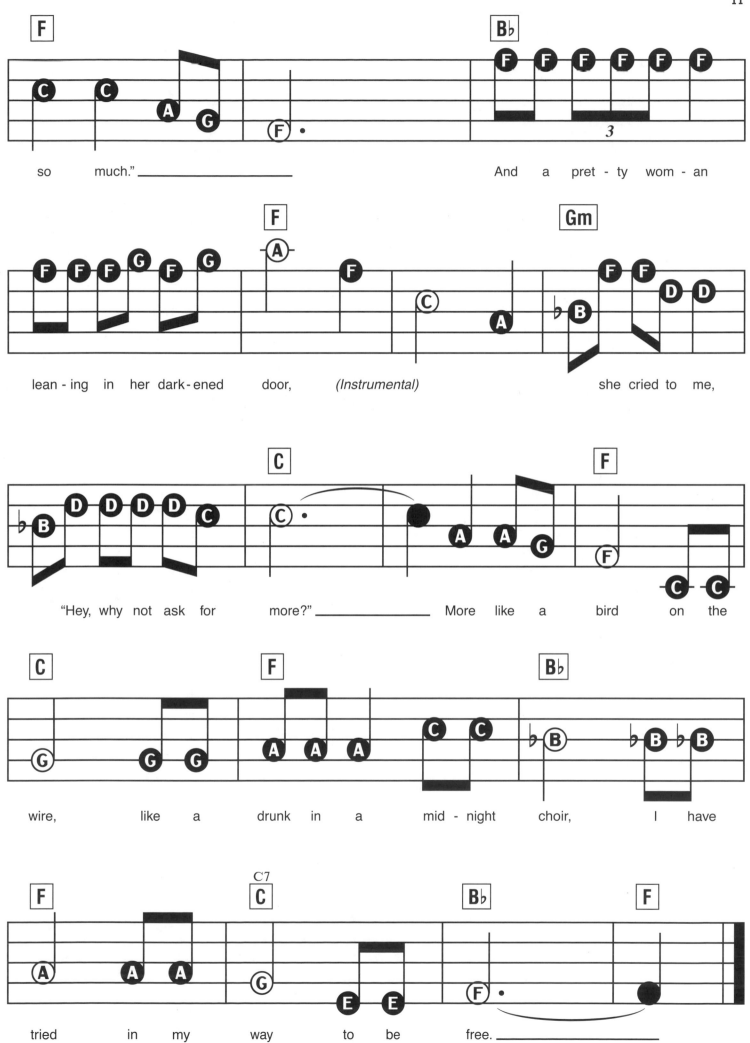

Chelsea Hotel #2

Registration 4
Rhythm: Waltz

Words and Music by
Leonard Cohen

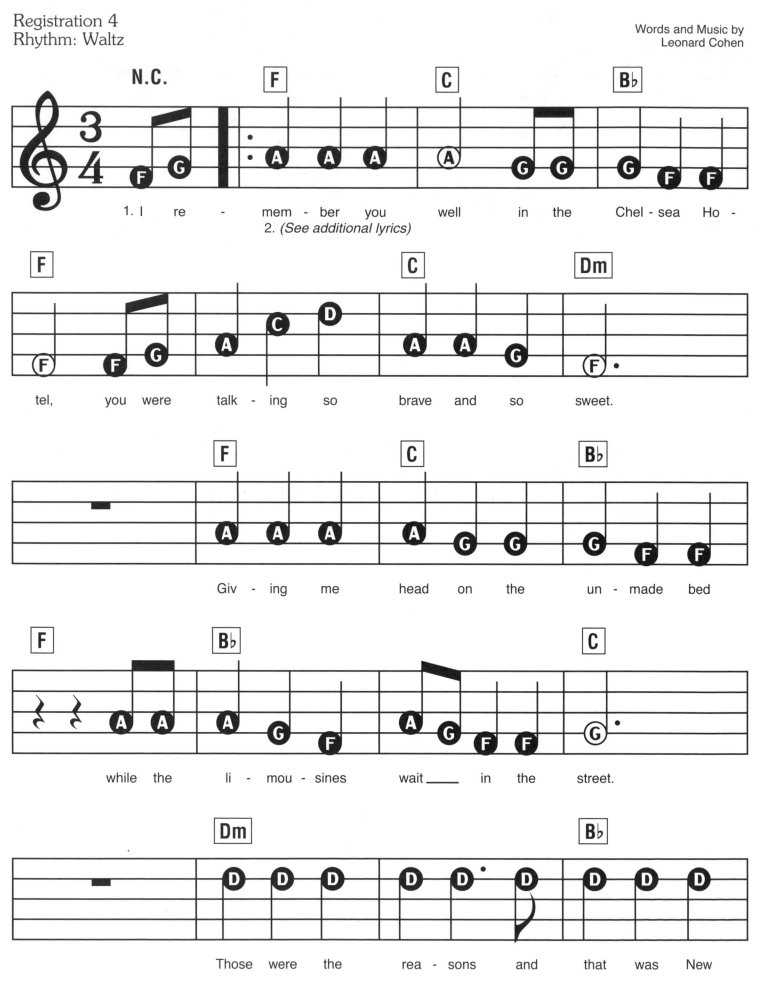

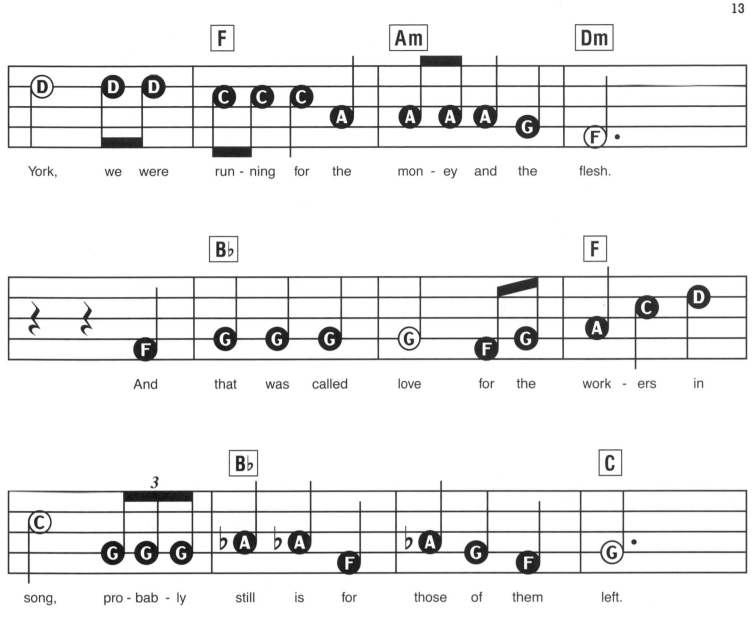

York, we were run - ning for the mon - ey and the flesh.

And that was called love for the work - ers in

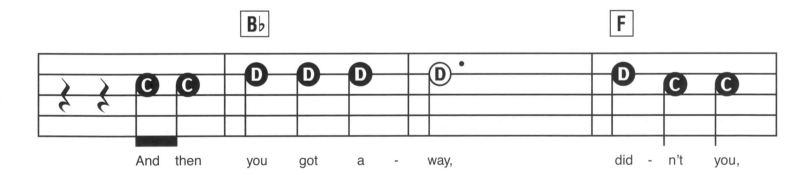

song, pro - bab - ly still is for those of them left.

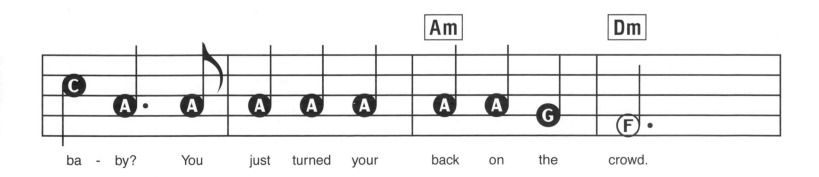

And then you got a - way, did - n't you,

ba - by? You just turned your back on the crowd.

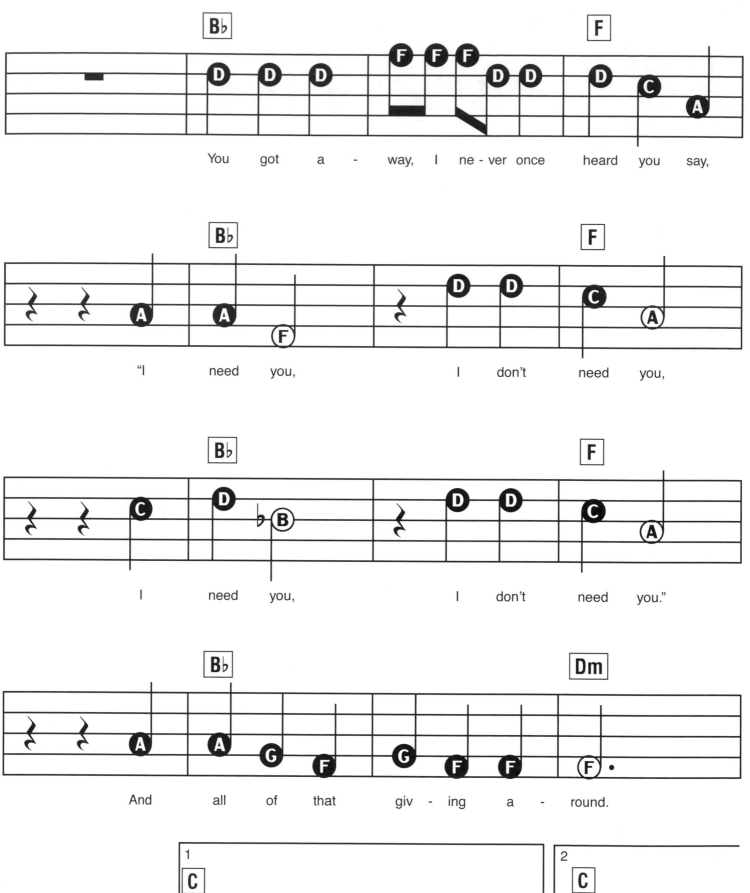

You got a - way, I ne - ver once heard you say,

"I need you, I don't need you,

I need you, I don't need you."

And all of that giv - ing a - round.

I re -

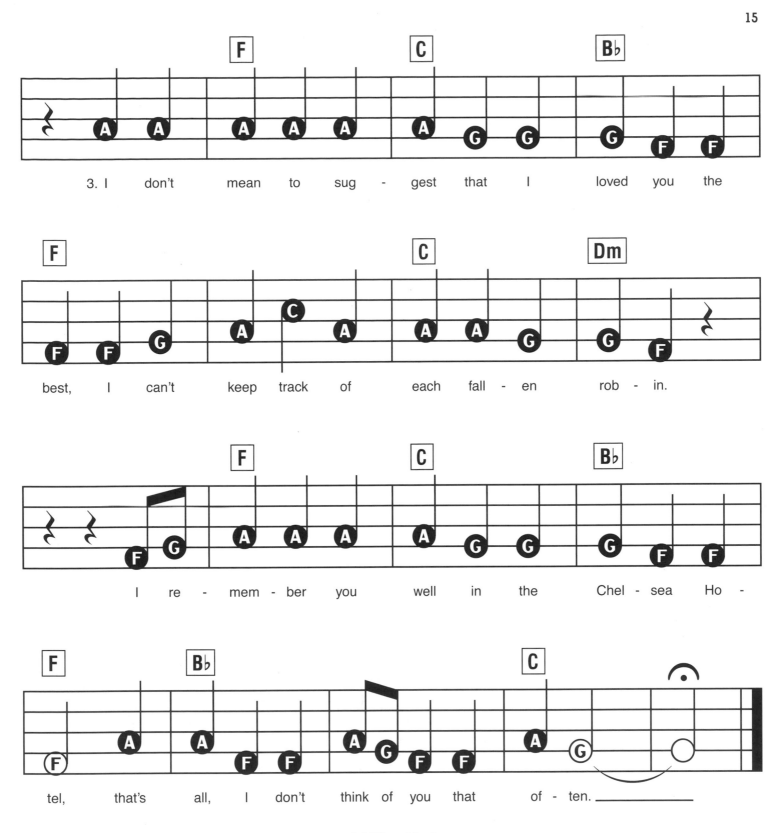

Additional Lyrics

2. I remember you well in the Chelsea Hotel,
   You were famous, your heart was a legend.
   You told me again you preferred handsome men,
   But for me you would make an exception.
   And clenching your fist for the ones like us
   Who are oppressed by the figures of beauty
   You fixed yourself. You said, "Well, never mind.
   We are ugly, but we have the music."

Dance Me to the End of Love

Registration 4
Rhythm: Fox Trot

Words and Music by
Leonard Cohen

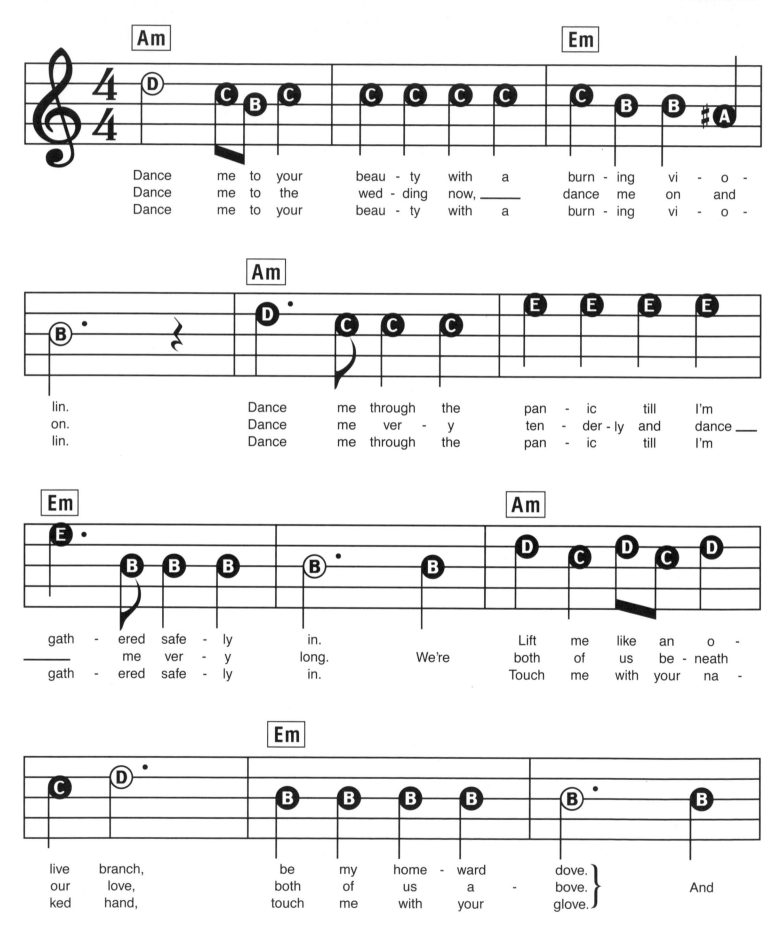

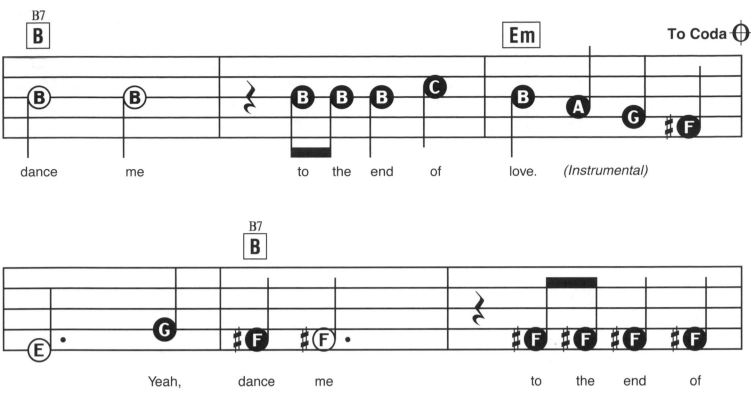

dance   me   to the end   of   love.   *(Instrumental)*

Yeah,   dance   me   to   the   end   of

love.

{ Let   me   see   your
{ Dance   me   to   the

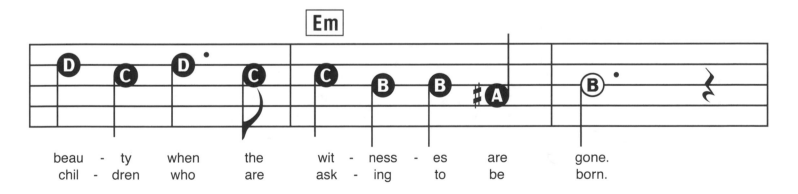

beau - ty   when   the   wit - ness - es   are   gone.
chil - dren   who   are   ask - ing   to   be   born.

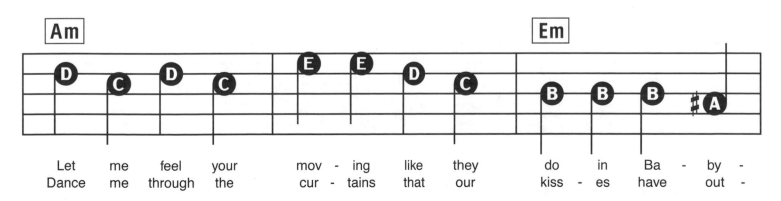

Let   me   feel   your   mov - ing   like   they   do   in   Ba - by -
Dance   me   through   the   cur - tains   that   our   kiss - es   have   out -

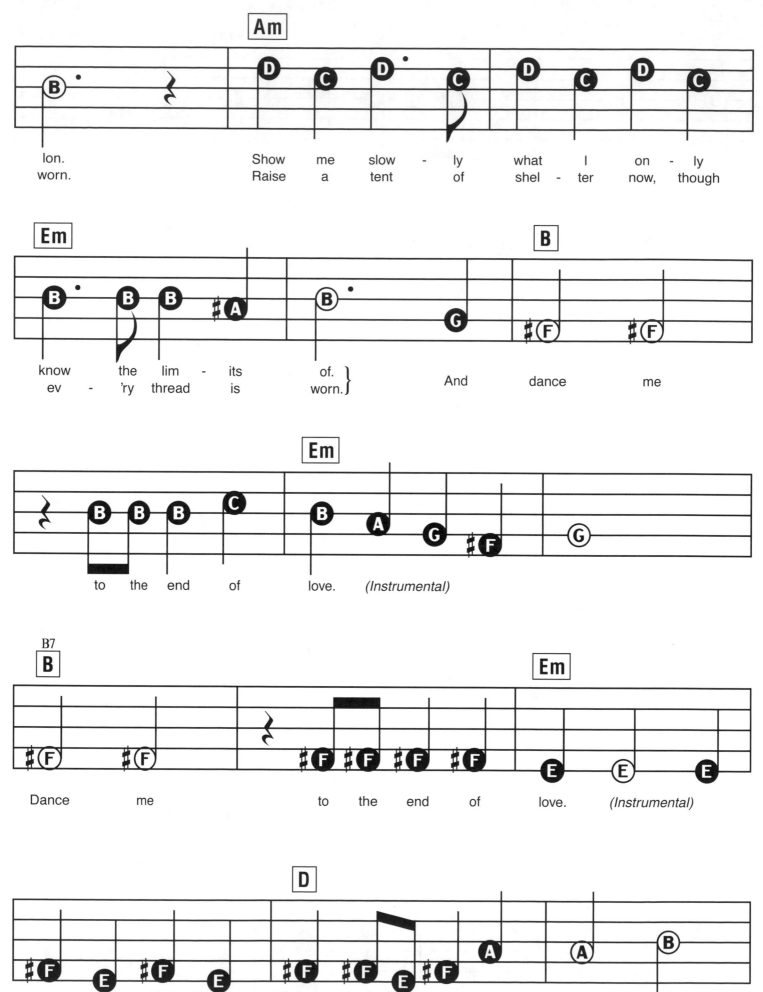

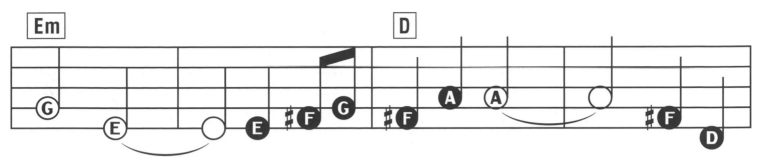

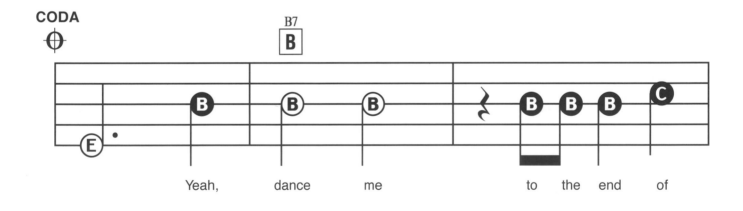

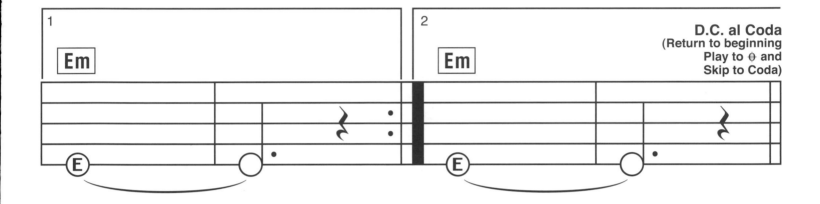

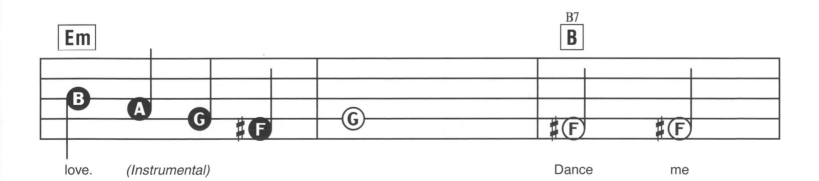

Yeah, dance me to the end of love. (Instrumental) Dance me

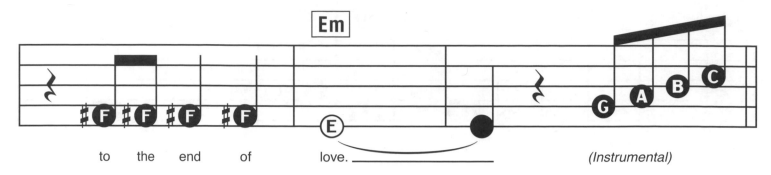

to   the   end   of   love. _____ *(Instrumental)*

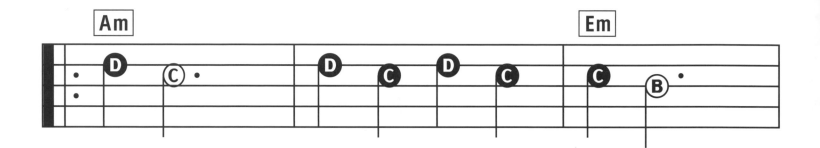

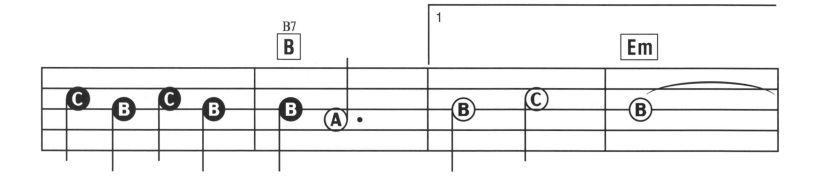

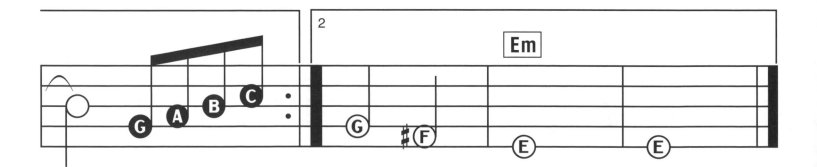

Famous Blue Raincoat

Registration 4
Rhythm: Waltz

Words and Music by
Leonard Cohen

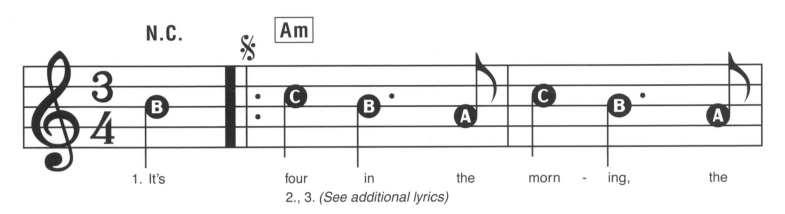

1. It's four in the morn - ing, the
2., 3. *(See additional lyrics)*

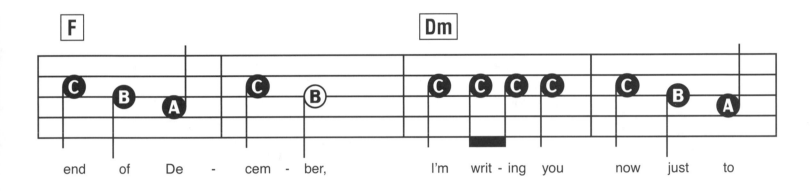

end of De - cem - ber, I'm writ - ing you now just to

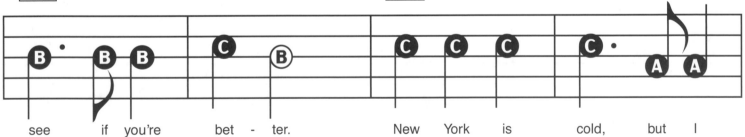

see if you're bet - ter. New York is cold, but I

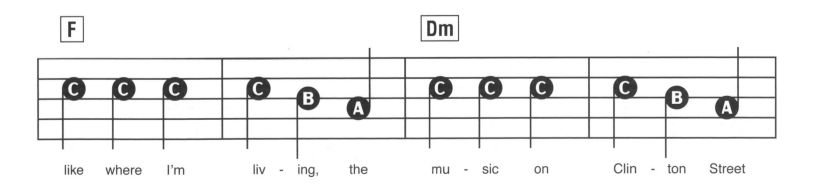

like where I'm liv - ing, the mu - sic on Clin - ton Street

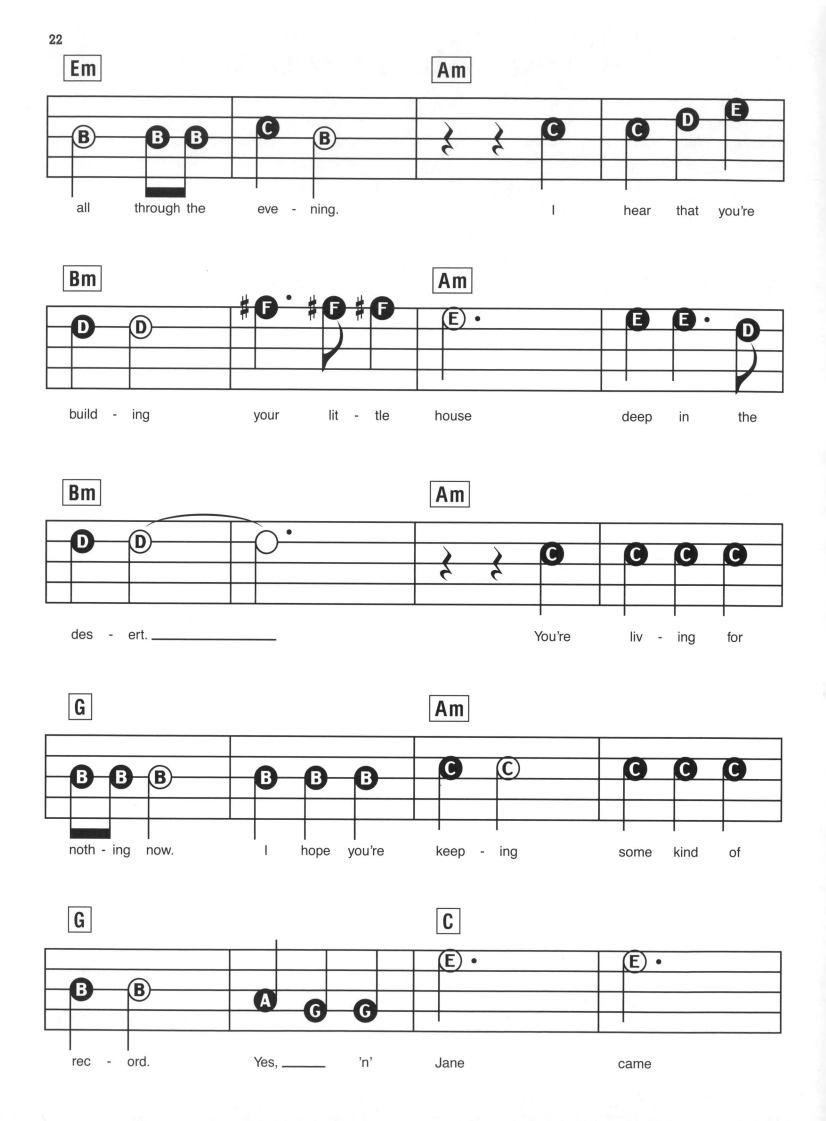

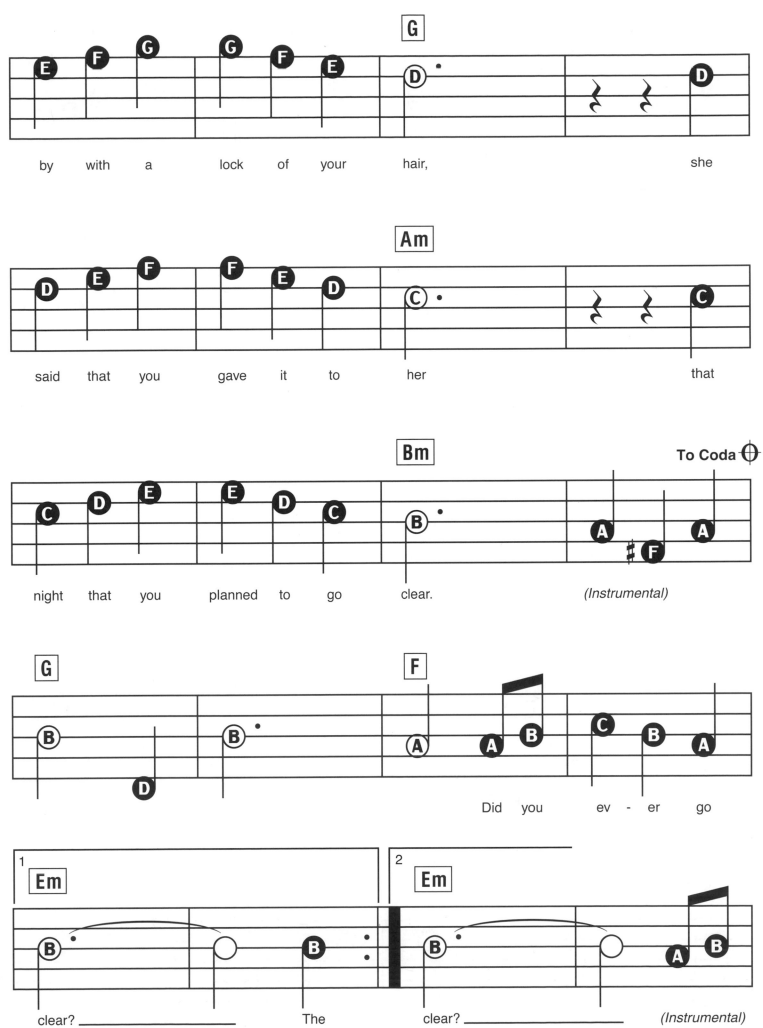

24

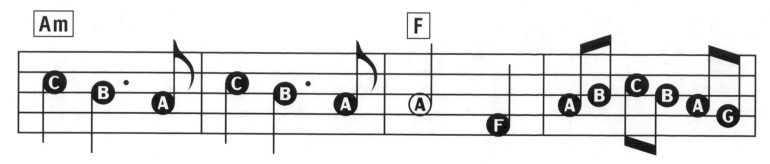

D.S. al Coda
(Return to ℅
Play to ⊕ and
Skip to Coda)

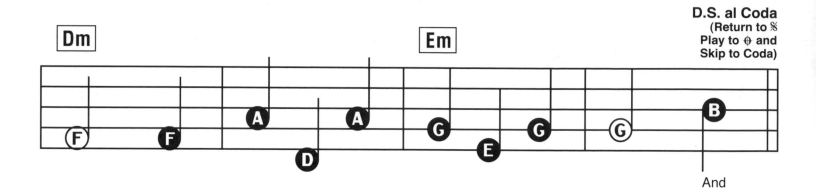

And

CODA

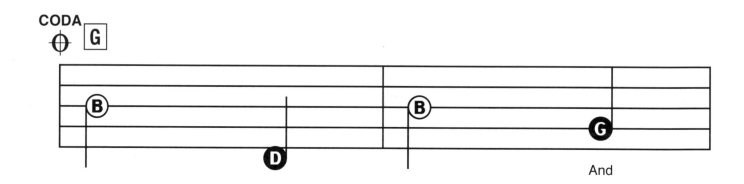

And

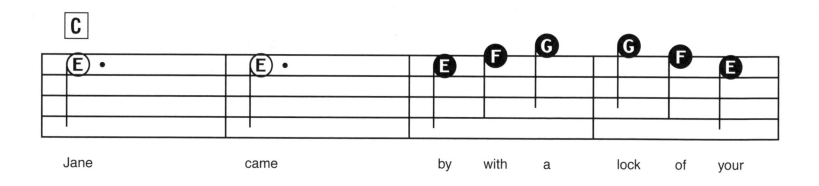

Jane   came   by   with   a   lock   of   your

hair,   she   said   that   you   gave   it   to

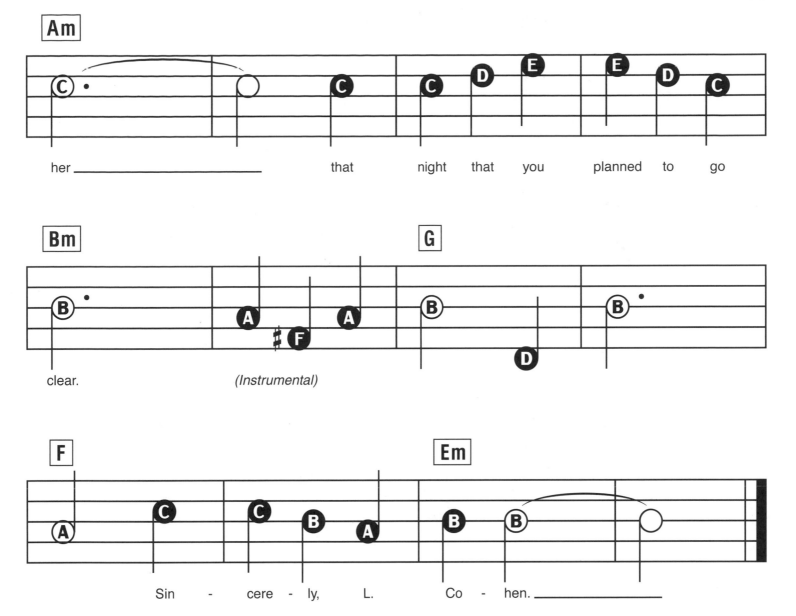

Additional Lyrics

2. The last time we saw you, you looked so much older.
   Your famous blue raincoat was torn at the shoulder.
   You'd been to the station to meet ev'ry train.
   You came home with Lili Marlene
   And treated my woman to a flake of your life,
   And when she came back, she was nobody's wife.

   Well, I see you there with a rose in your teeth,
   One more thin gypsy thief.
   Well, I see Jane's away, she sends her regards.

3. And what can I tell my brother, my killer?
   What can I possibly say?
   I guess that I miss you, I guess I forgive you,
   I'm glad you stood in my way.
   If you ever come by here for Jane or for me,
   Well, your enemy is sleeping and his woman is free.

   Yes, thanks for the trouble you took from her eyes.
   I thought it was there for good, so I never tried.

Everybody Knows

Registration 4
Rhythm: Pop or Rock

Words and Music by Leonard Cohen
and Sharon Robinson

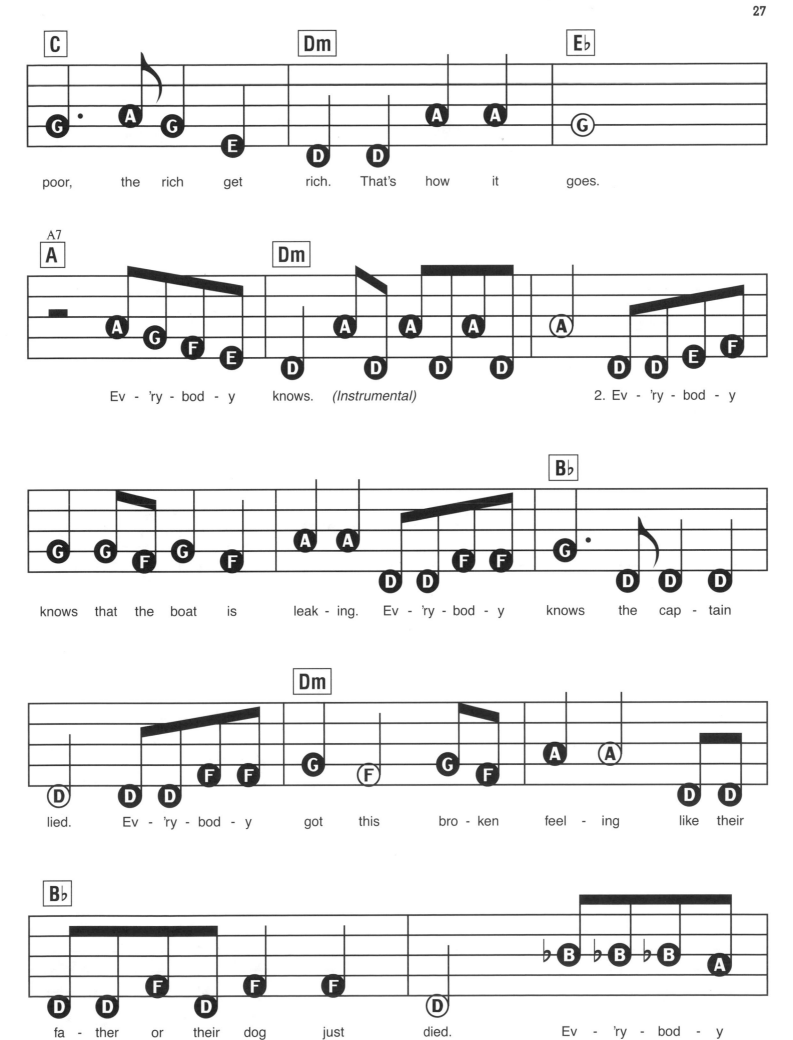

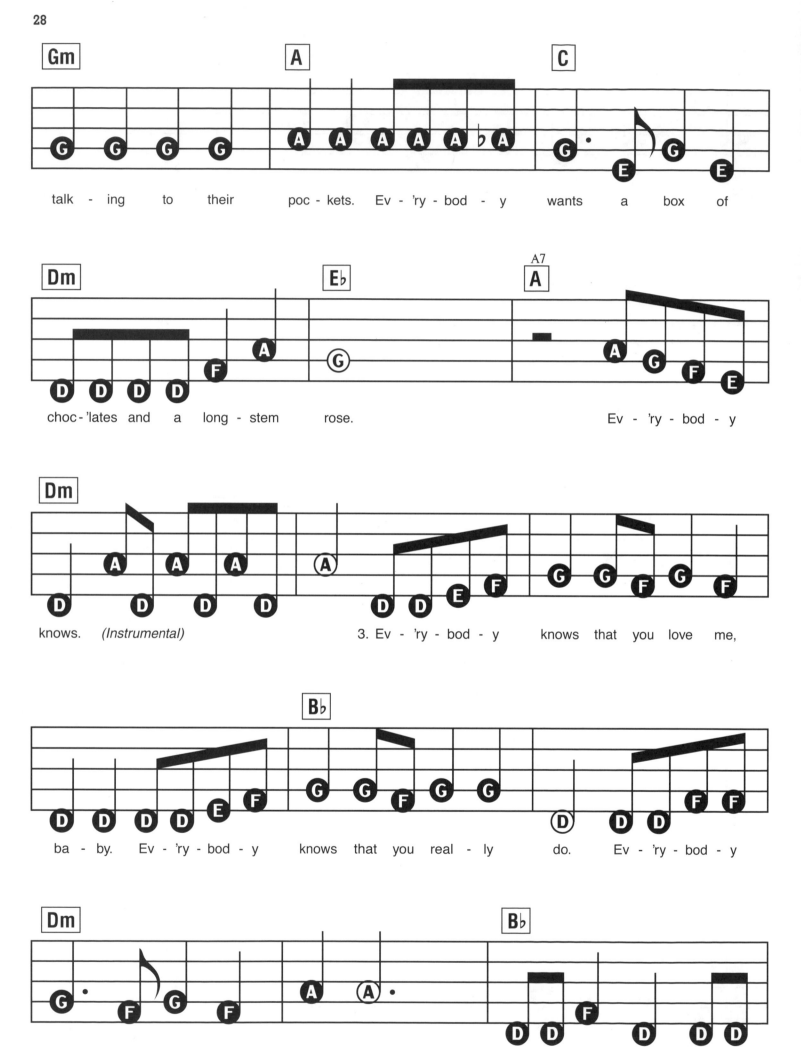

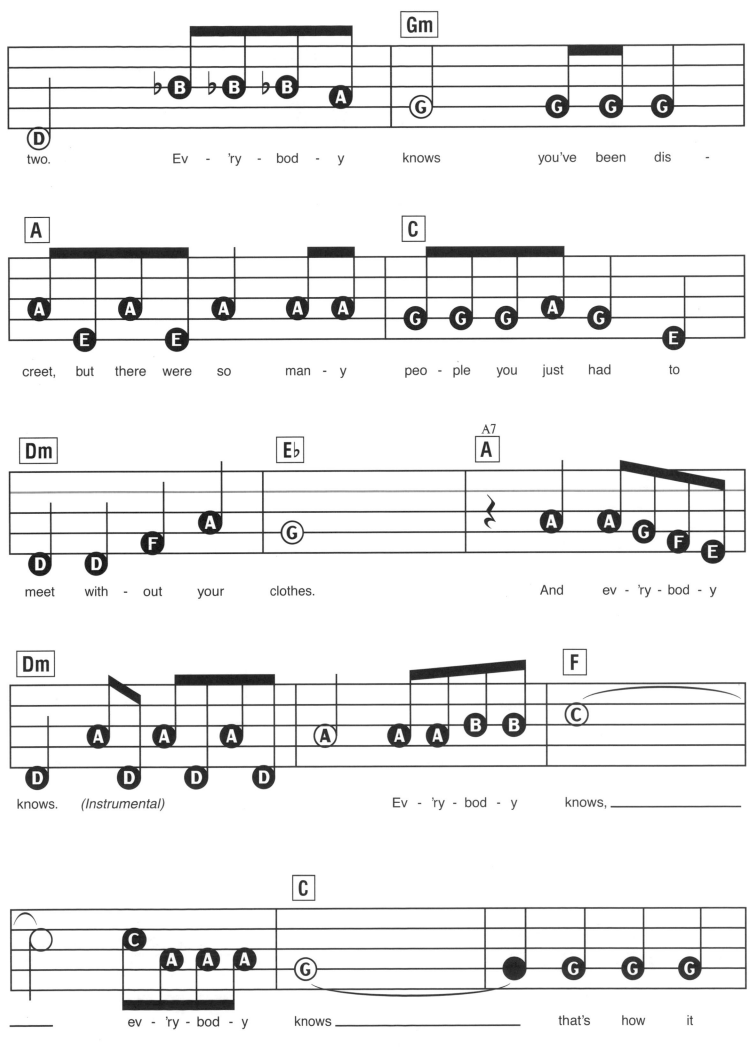

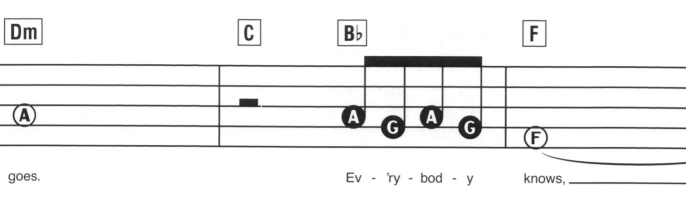

goes.　　　　　　Ev - 'ry - bod - y　　knows,

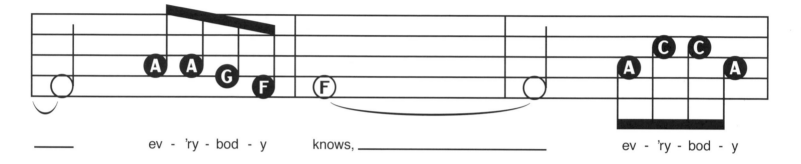

ev - 'ry - bod - y　　knows,　　　　　　ev - 'ry - bod - y

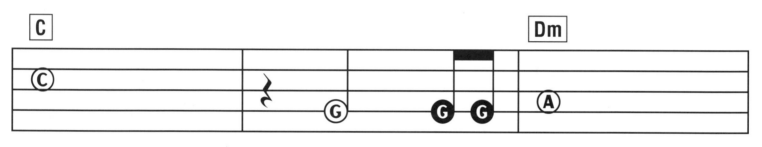

knows　　　　　that's　　how　it　goes.

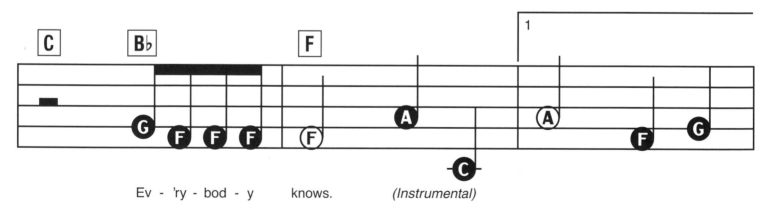

Ev - 'ry - bod - y　knows.　　(Instrumental)

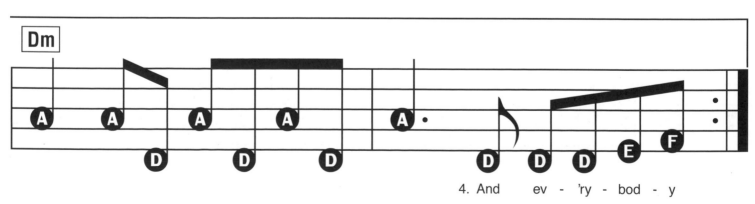

4. And　ev - 'ry - bod - y

Ev - 'ry - bod - y knows, _____ ev - 'ry - bod - y

knows that's how it goes.

Oh, ev - 'ry - bod - y knows.

Additional Lyrics

4. And everybody knows that it's now or never.
   Everybody knows that it's me or you.
   And everybody knows that you live forever
   When you've done a line or two.
   Everybody knows the deal is rotten:
   Old Black Joe's still pickin' cotton
   For your ribbons and bows. And everybody knows.

5. Everybody knows that the plague is coming.
   Everybody knows that it's moving fast.
   Everybody knows that the naked man and woman
   Are just a shining artifact of the past.
   Everybody knows that the scene is dead,
   But there's gonna be a meter on your bed
   That will disclose what everybody knows.

6. And everybody knows that you're in trouble.
   Everybody knows what you've been through,
   From the bloody cross on top of Calvary
   To the beach of Malibu.
   Everybody knows it's coming apart:
   Take one last look at this Sacred Heart
   Before it blows. And everybody knows.

First We Take Manhattan

Registration 4
Rhythm: Dance or Rock

Words and Music by
Leonard Cohen

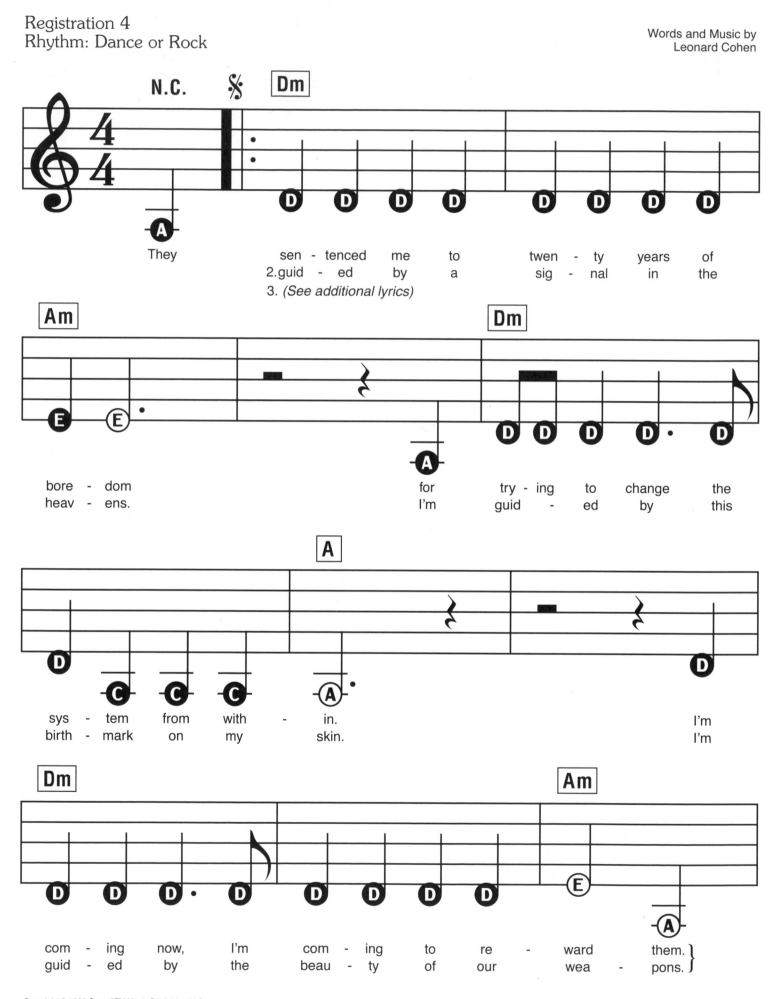

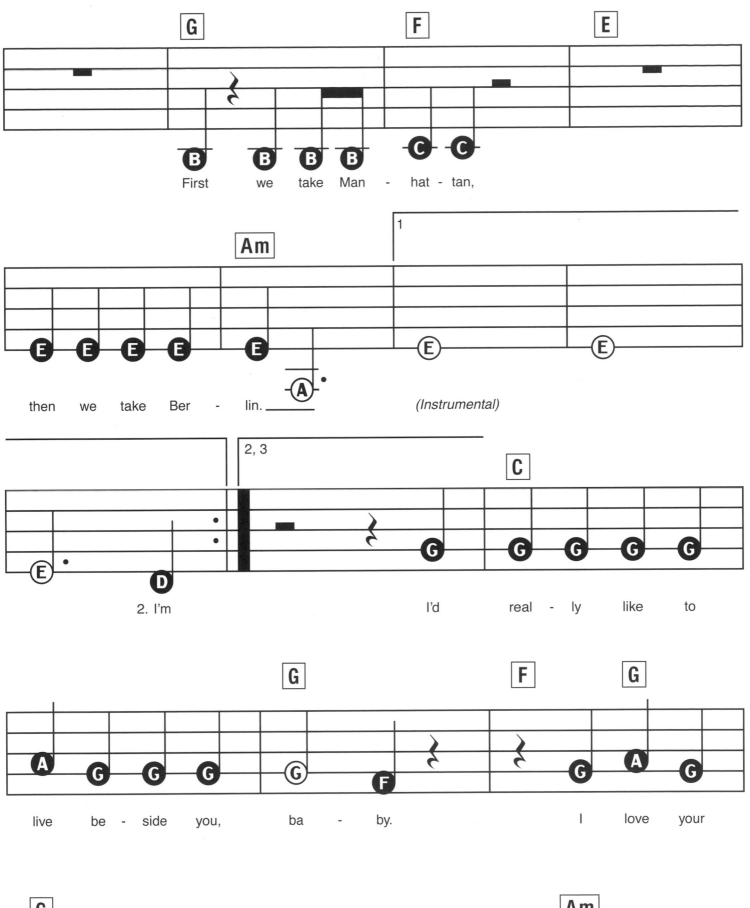

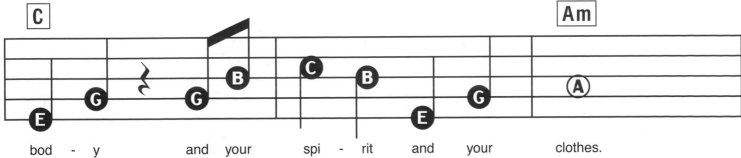

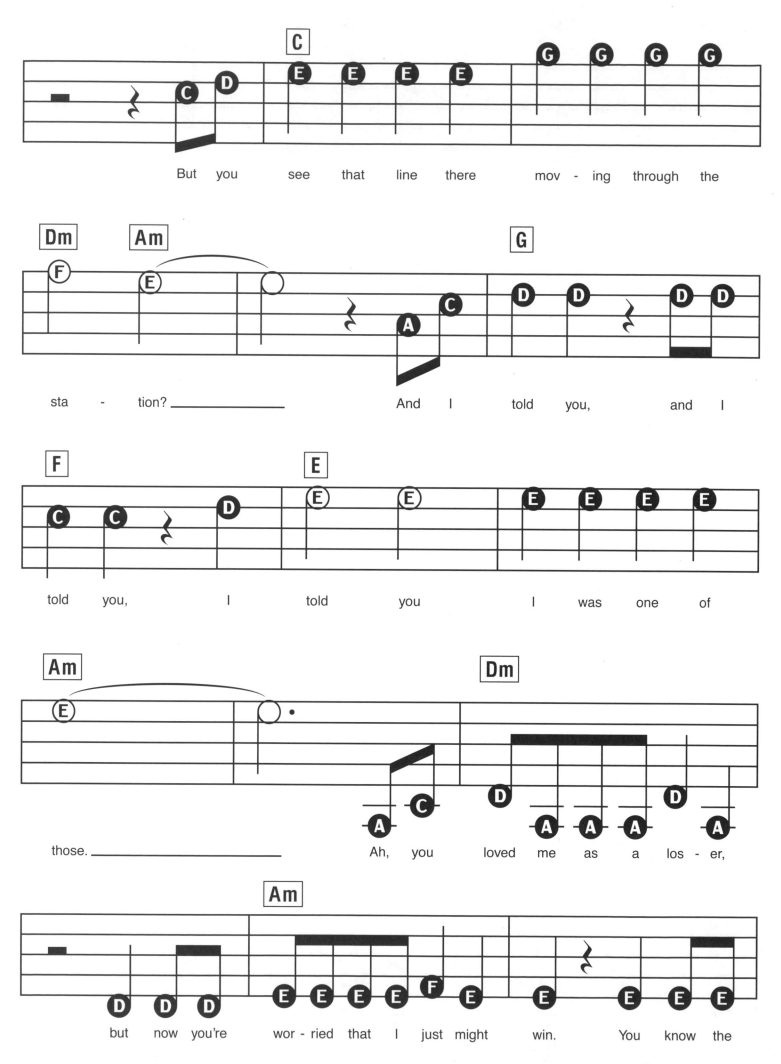

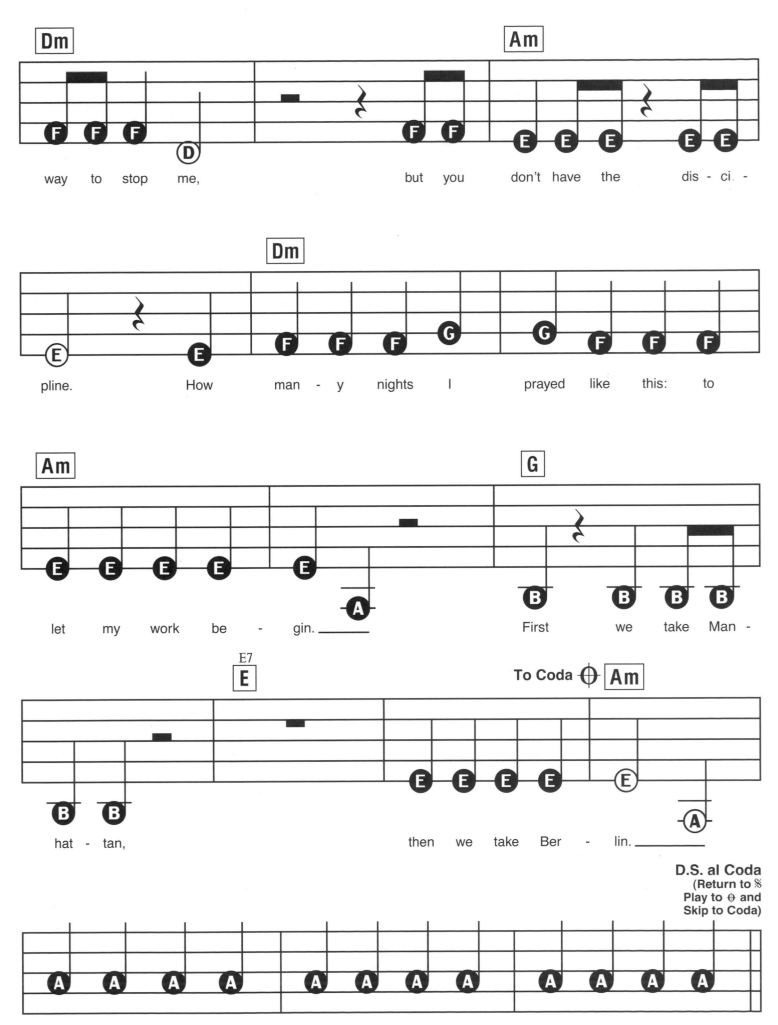

(Instrumental)

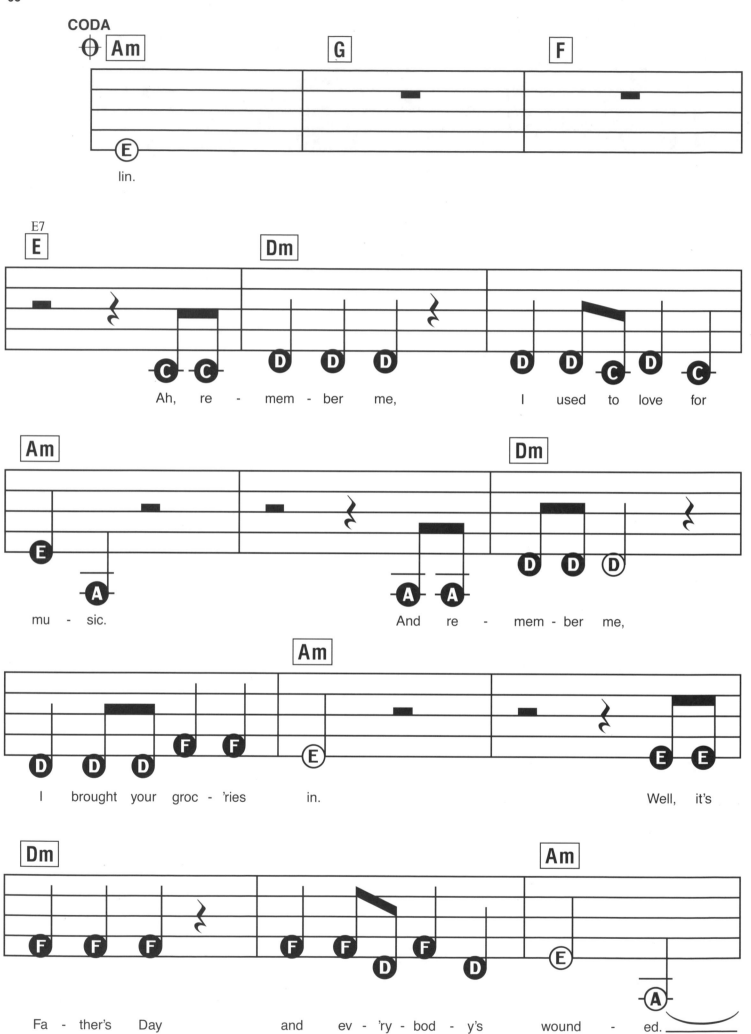

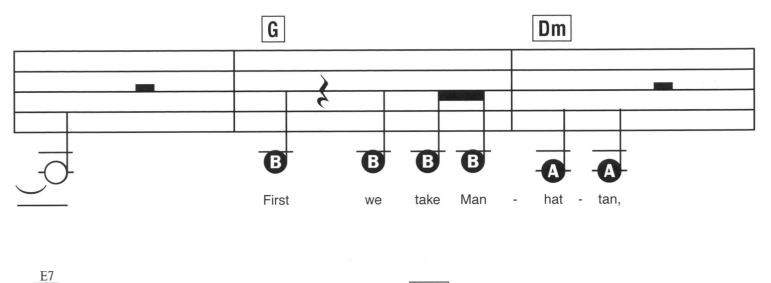

First   we   take   Man - hat - tan,

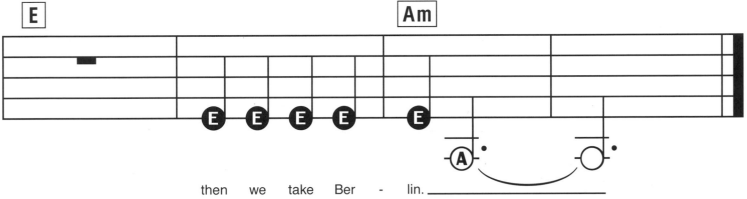

then   we   take   Ber - lin. _____

Additional Lyrics

3. I don't like your fashion business, mister.
   I don't like these drugs that keep you thin.
   I don't like what happened to my sister.
   First we take Manhattan, then we take Berlin.

   I'd really like to live beside you, baby.
   I love your body and your spirit and your clothes.
   But you see that line there moving throught the station?
   And I told you, and I told you,
   I told you I was one of those.

   And I thank you for those items that you sent me:
   The monkey and the plywood violin.
   I practiced every night and now I'm ready.
   First we take Manhattan, then we take Berlin.

The Future

Registration 8
Rhythm: Latin Rock

Words and Music by
Leonard Cohen

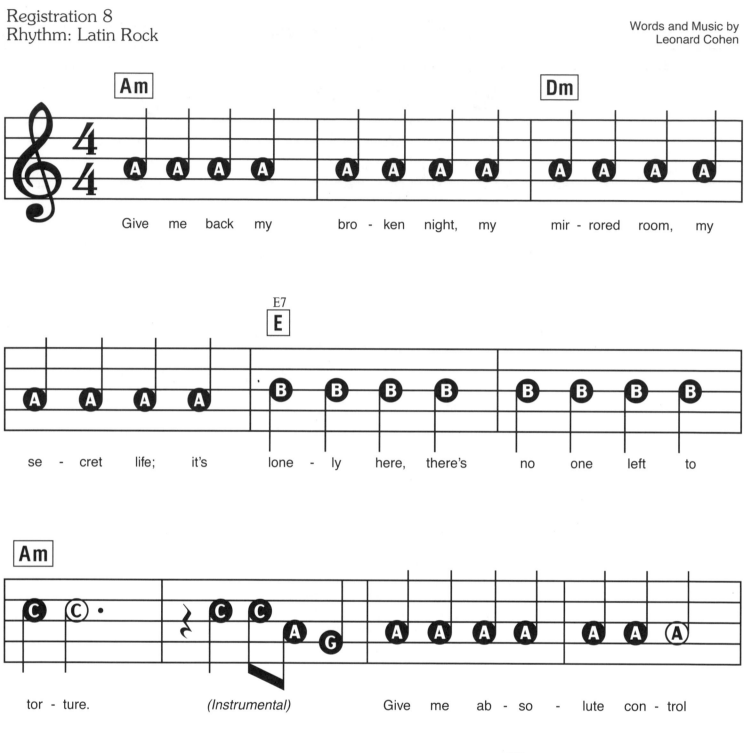

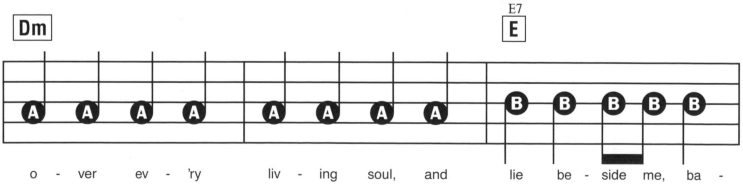

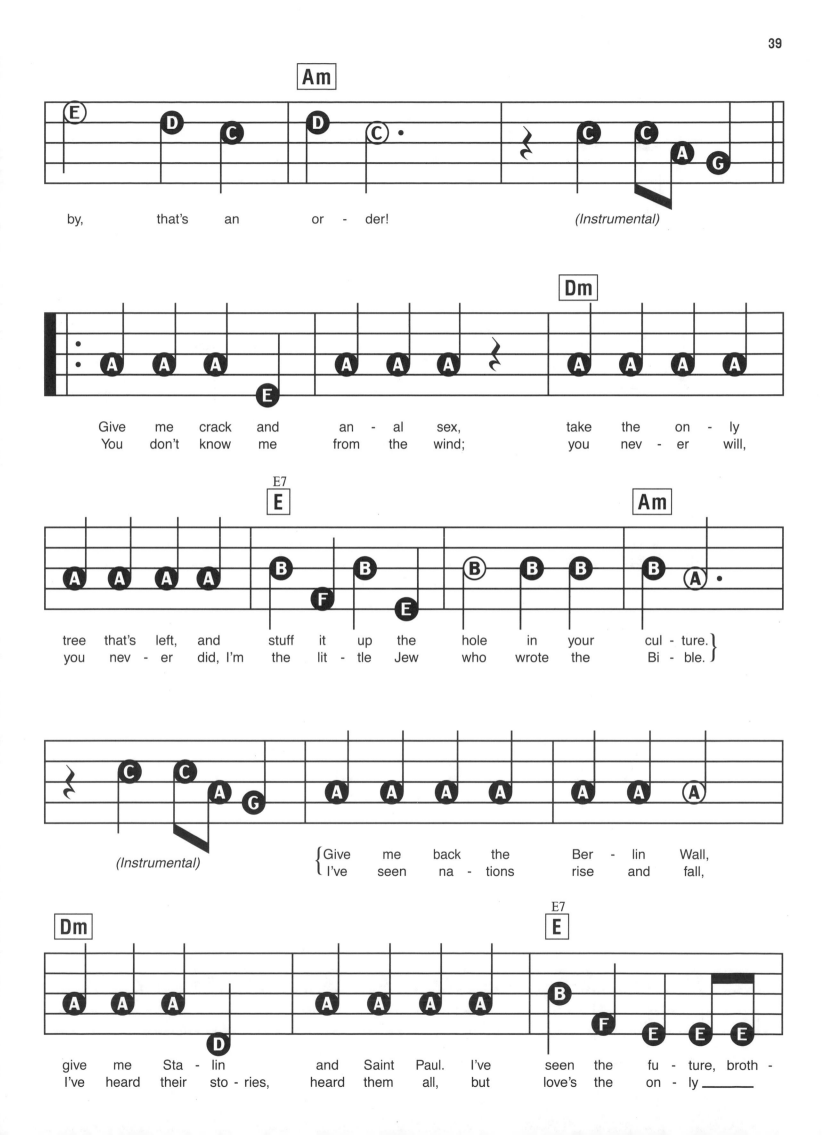

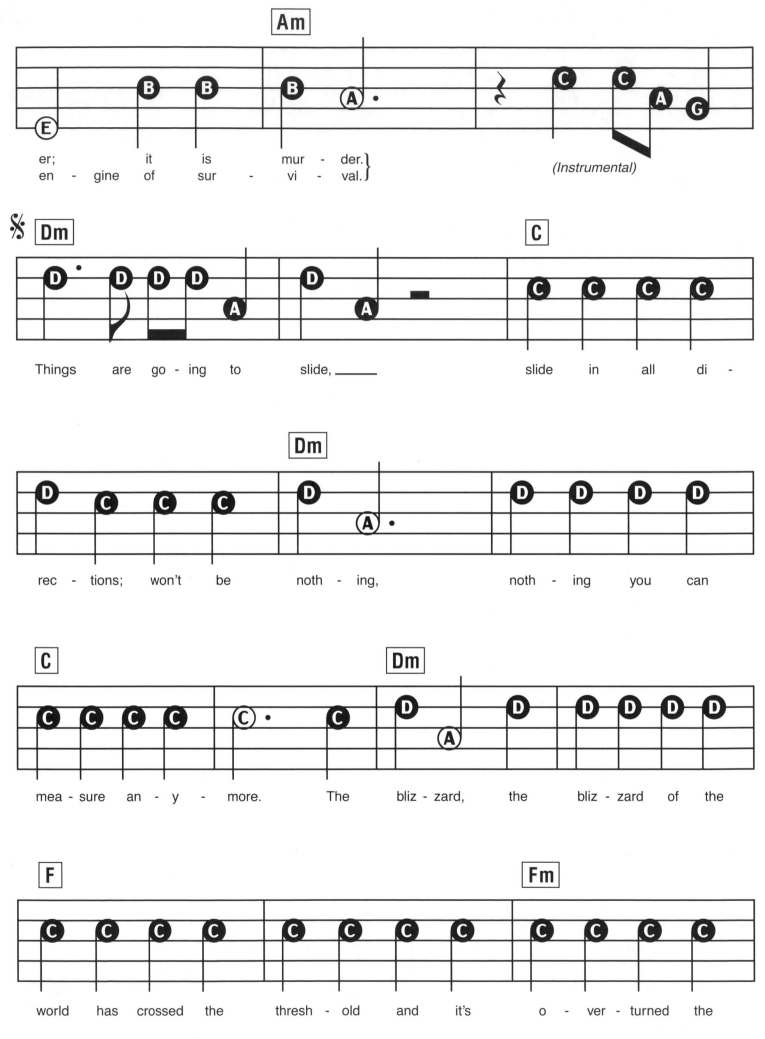

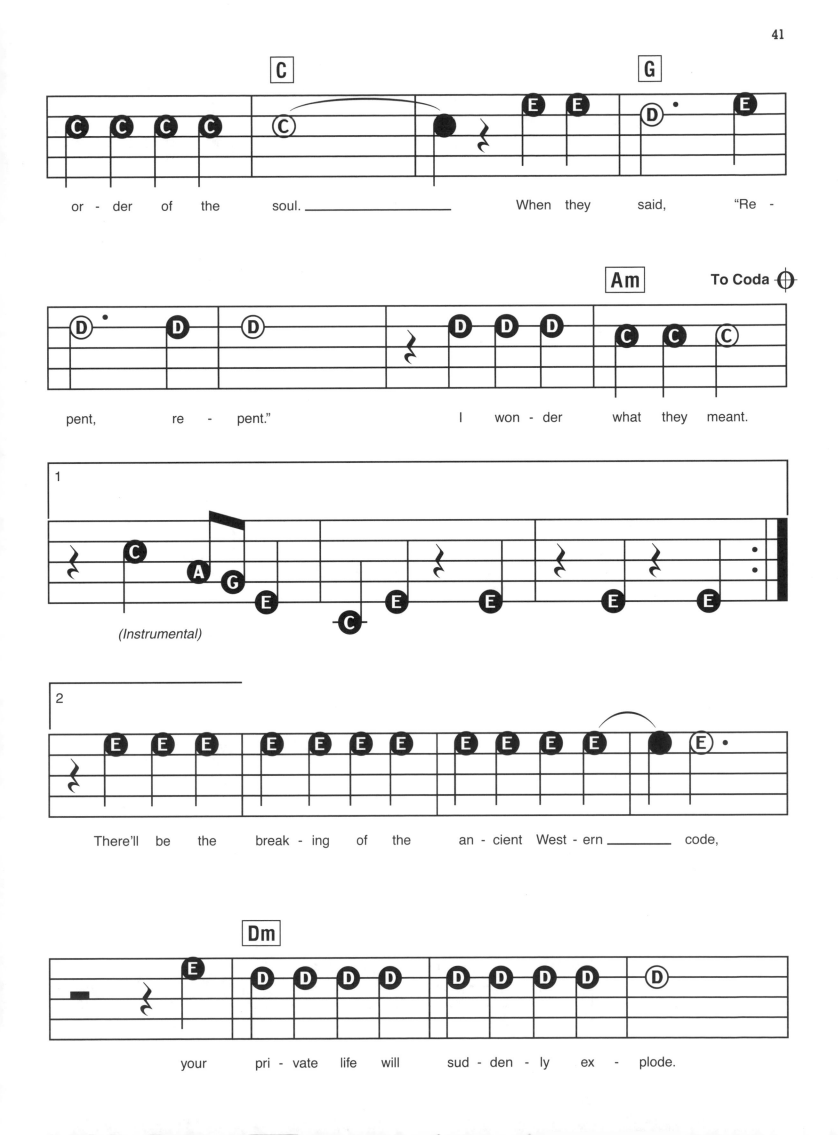

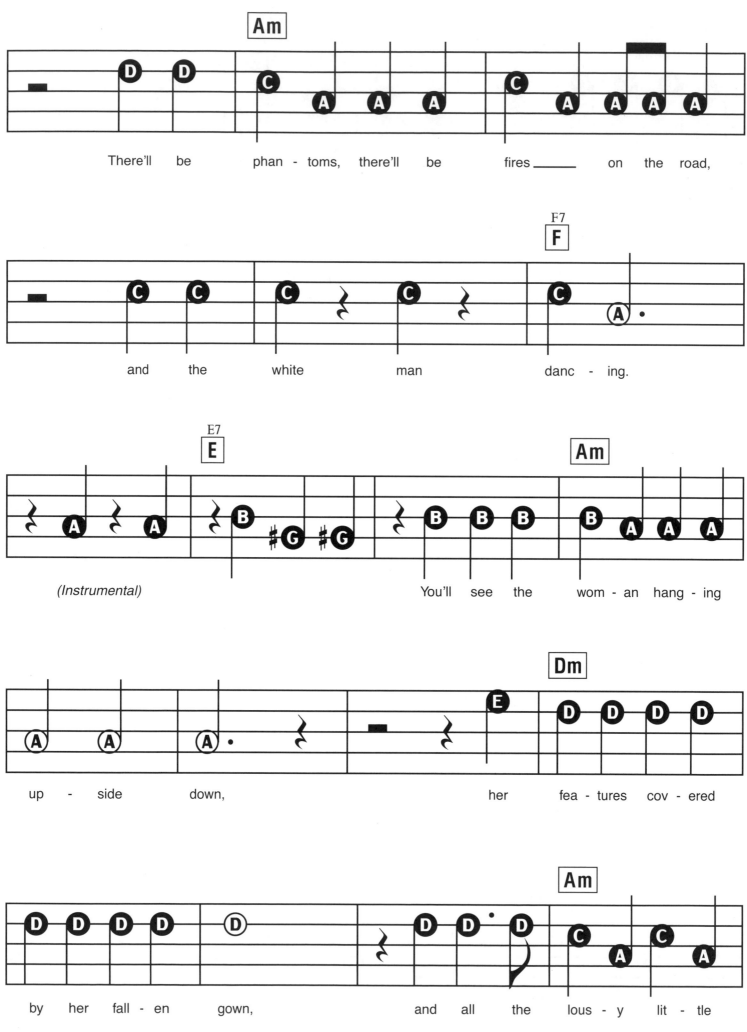

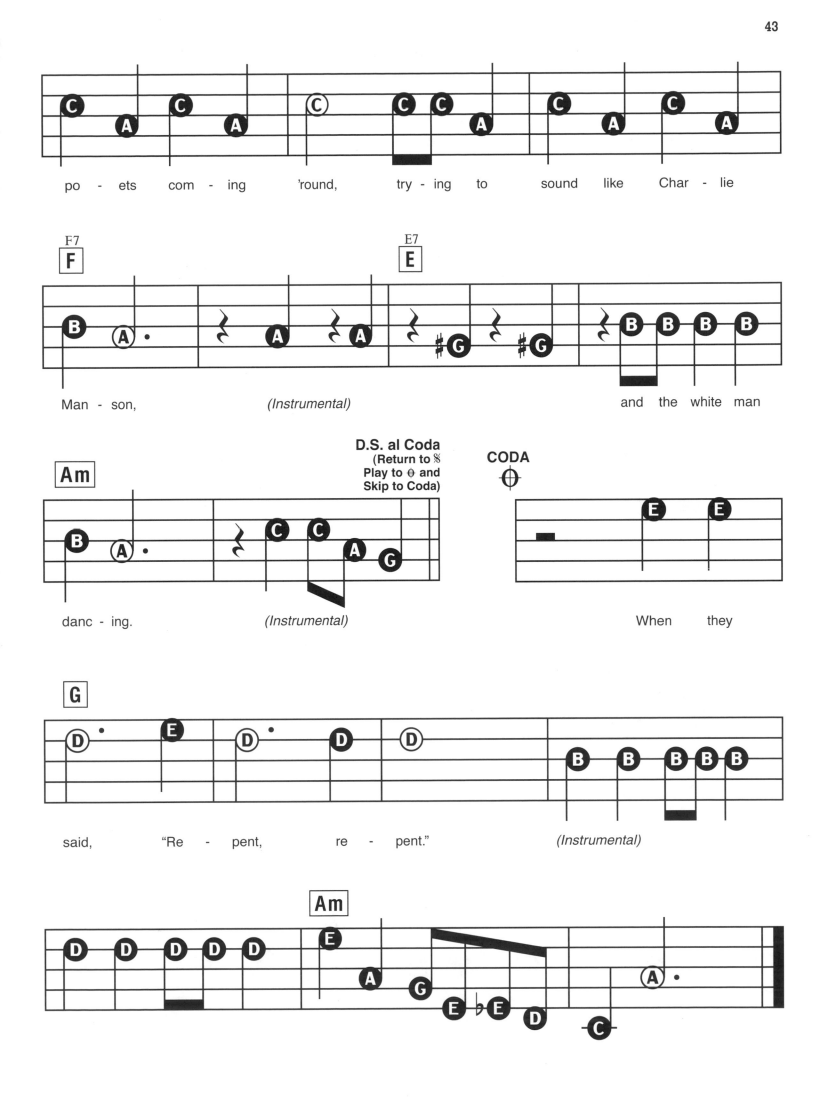

Hallelujah

Registration 4
Rhythm: 6/8 March

Words and Music by
Leonard Cohen

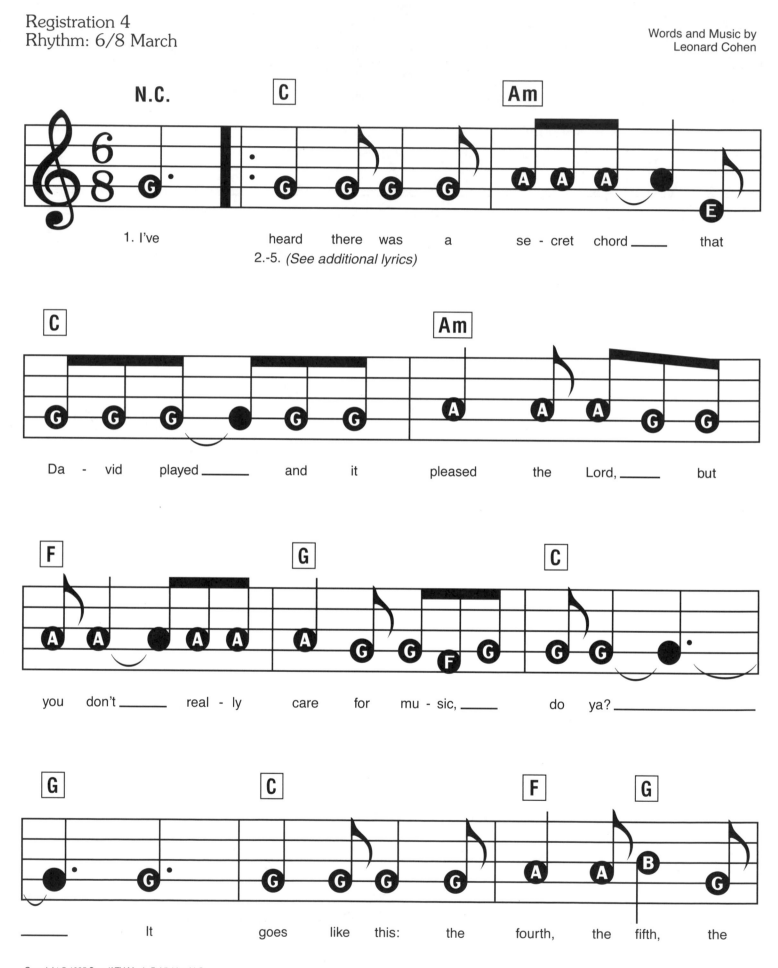

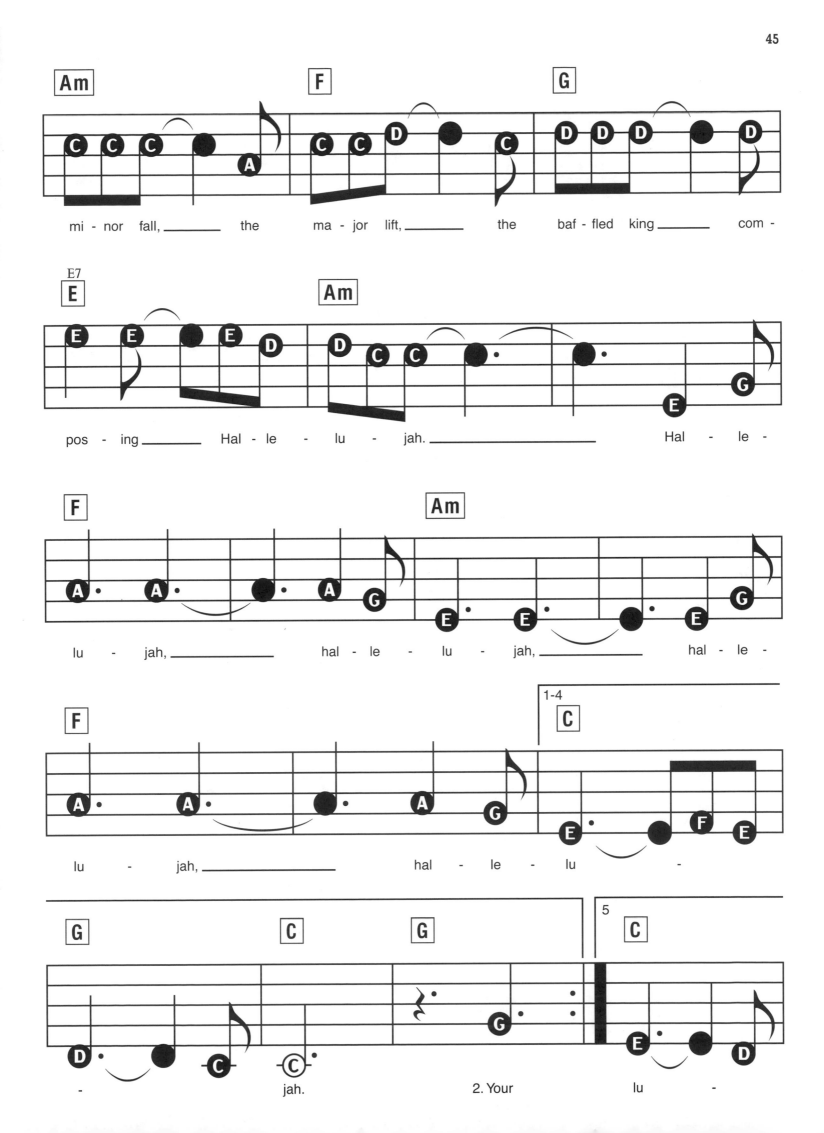

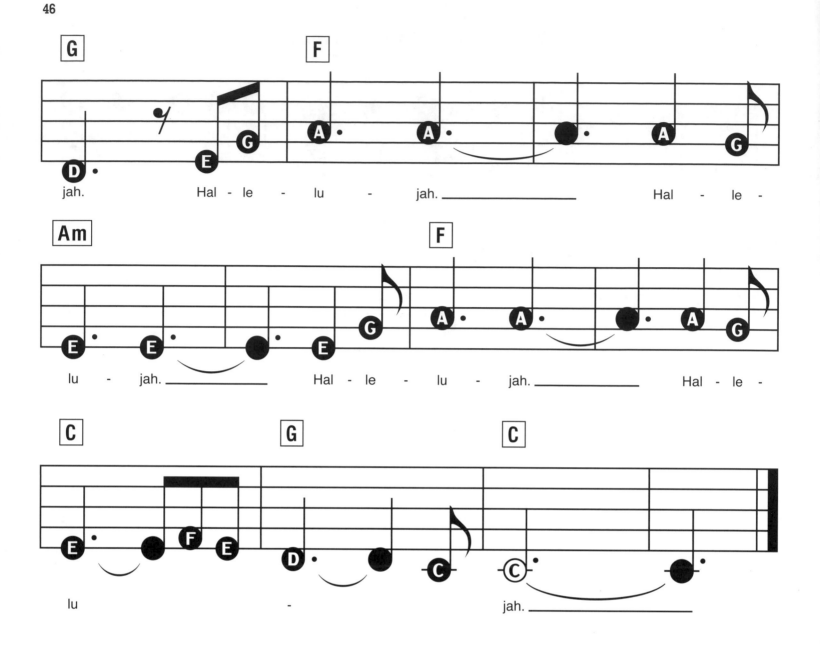

Additional Lyrics

2. Your faith was strong but you needed proof.
   You saw her bathing on the roof.
   Her beauty and the moonlight overthrew ya.
   She tied you to a kitchen chair.
   She broke your throne, she cut your hair.
   And from your lips she drew the Hallelujah.

3. Maybe I have been here before.
   I know this room, I've walked this floor.
   I used to live alone before I knew ya.
   I've seen your flag on the marble arch.
   Love is not a vict'ry march.
   It's a cold and it's a broken Hallelujah.

4. There was a time you let me know
   What's real and going on below.
   But now you never show it to me, do ya?
   And remember when I moved in you.
   The holy dark was movin', too,
   And every breath we drew was Hallelujah.

5. Maybe there's a God above,
   And all I ever learned from love
   Was how to shoot at someone who outdrew ya.
   And it's not a cry you can hear at night.
   It's not somebody who's seen the light.
   It's a cold and it's a broken Hallelujah.

I'm Your Man

Registration 4
Rhythm: Fox Trot or Swing

Words and Music by
Leonard Cohen

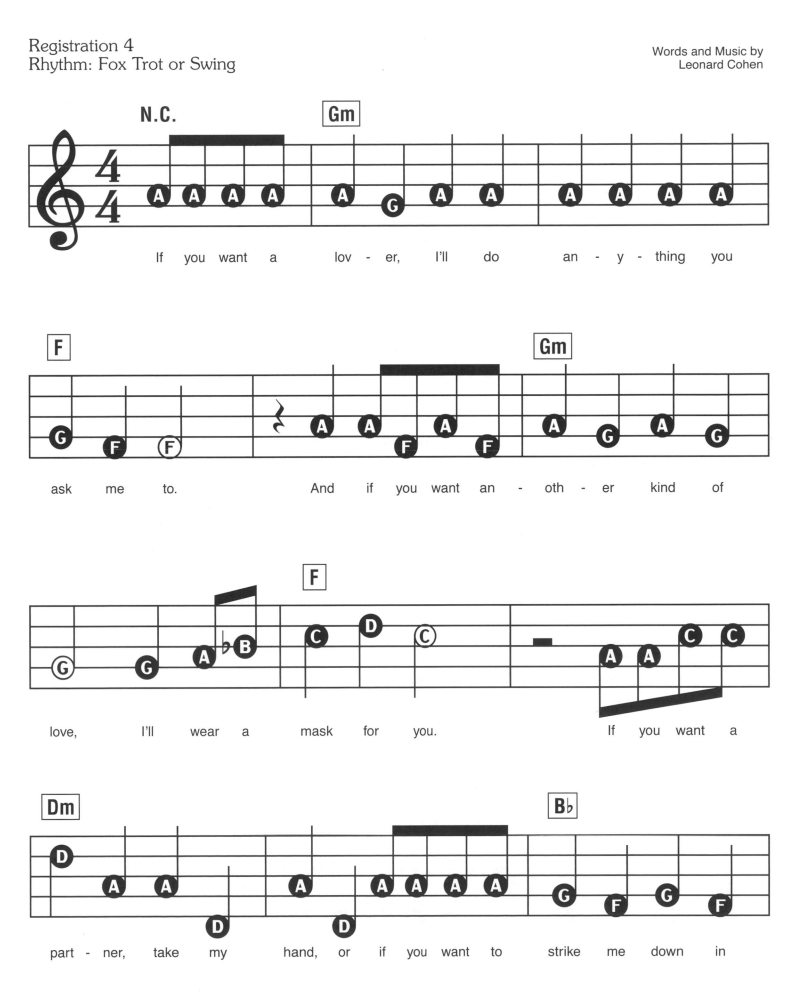

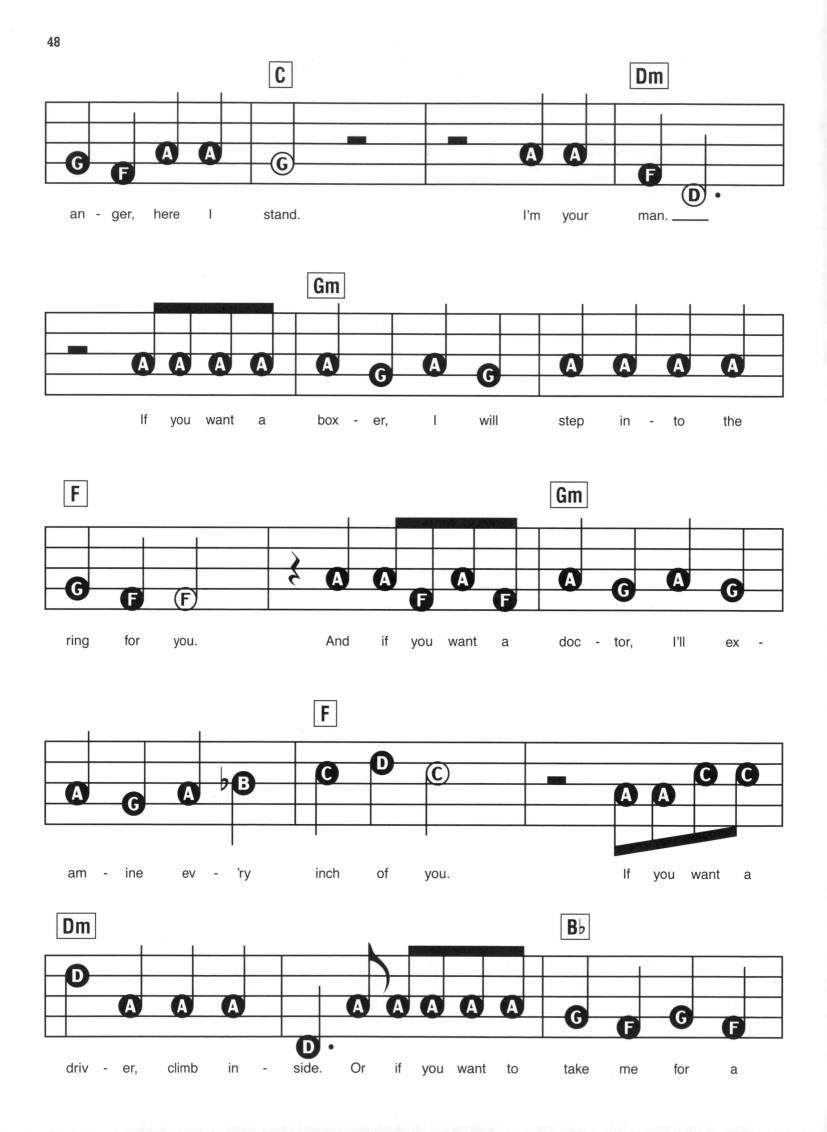

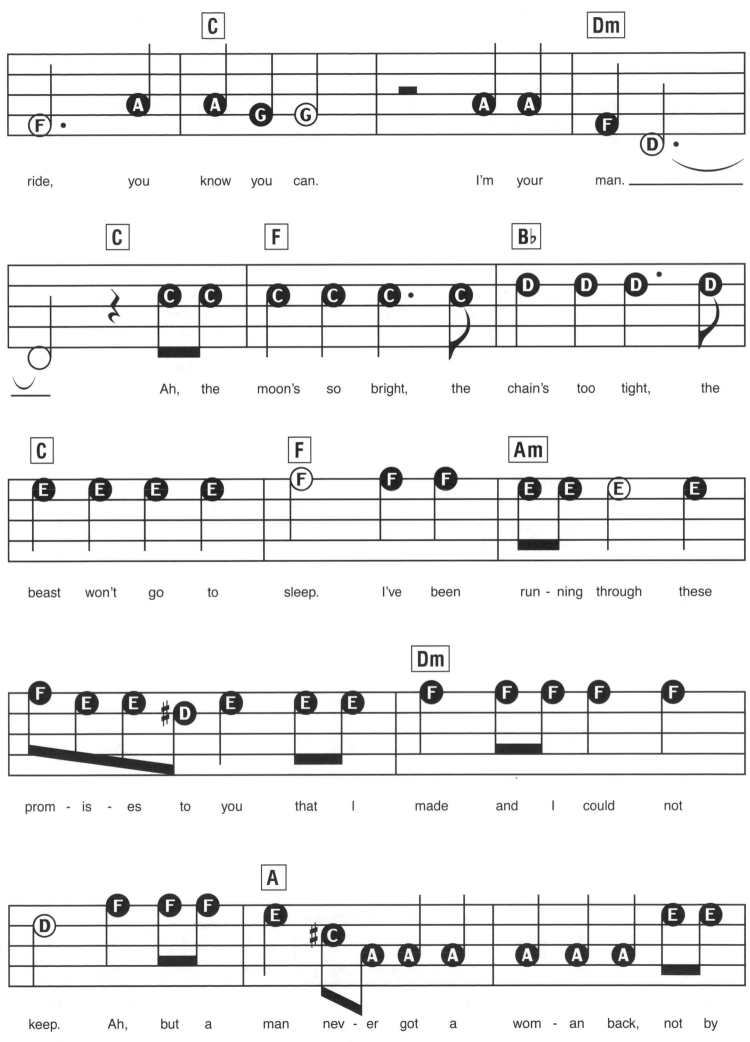

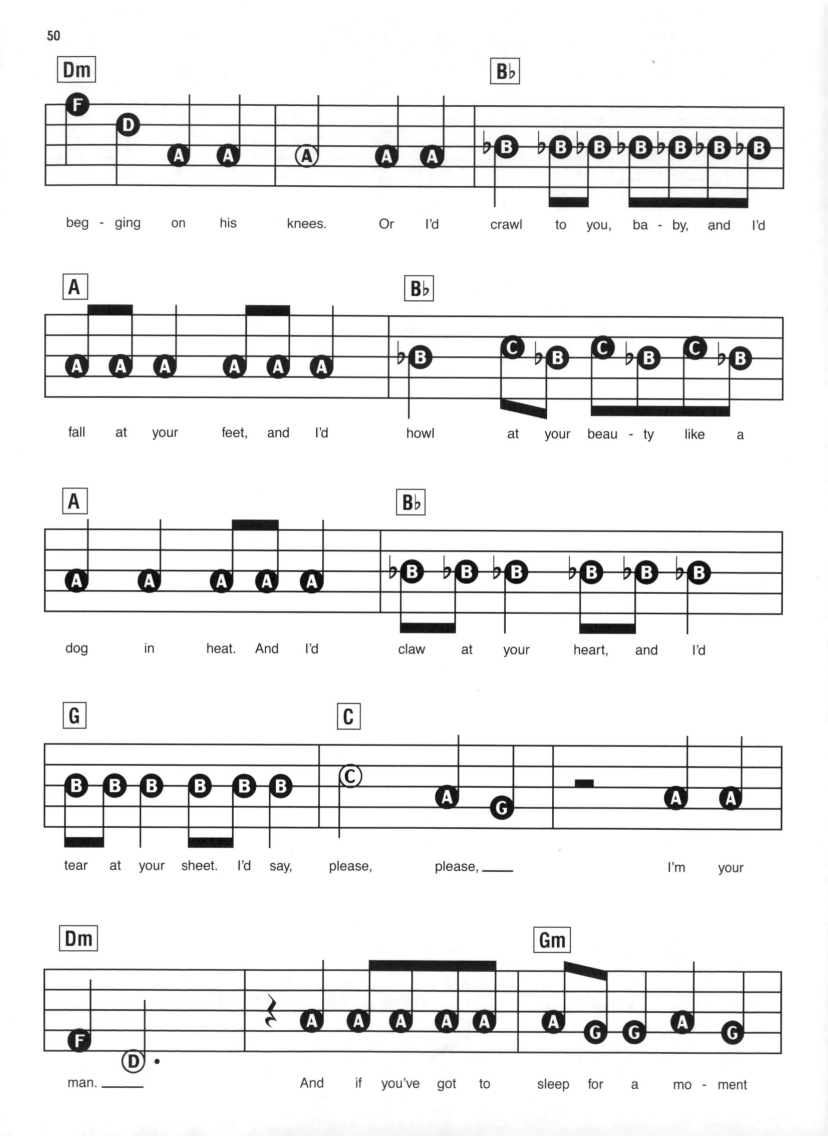

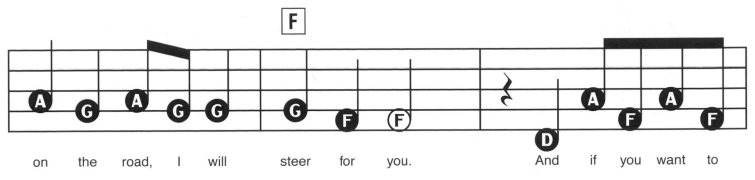

on the road, I will steer for you. And if you want to

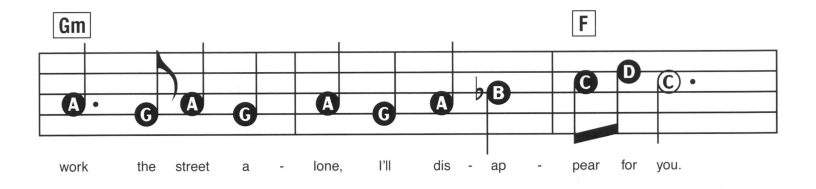

work the street a - lone, I'll dis - ap - pear for you.

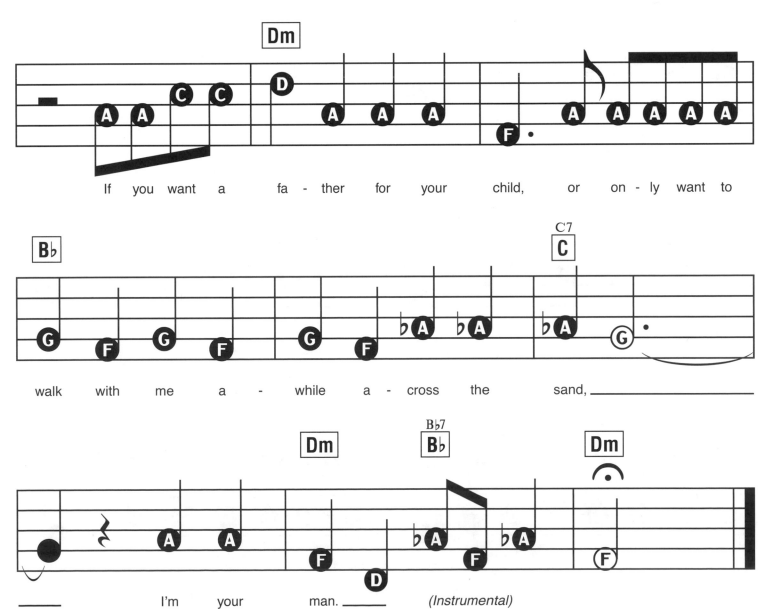

If you want a fa - ther for your child, or on - ly want to

walk with me a - while a - cross the sand,

I'm your man. _____ (Instrumental)

Hey, That's No Way to Say Goodbye

Registration 4
Rhythm: Folk

Words and Music by
Leonard Cohen

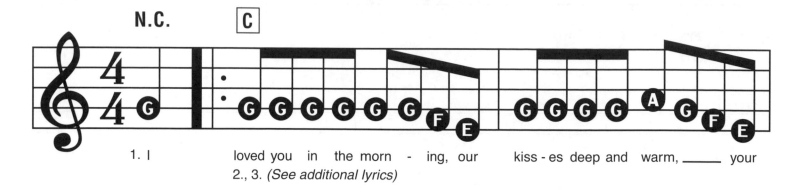

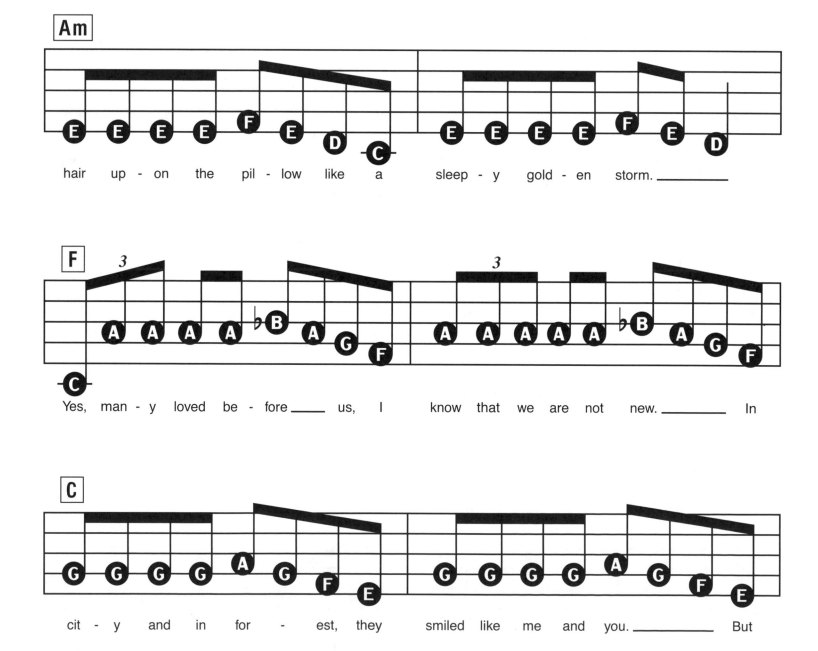

1. I loved you in the morn - ing, our kiss - es deep and warm, _____ your
2., 3. *(See additional lyrics)*

hair up - on the pil - low like a sleep - y gold - en storm. _____

Yes, man - y loved be - fore _____ us, I know that we are not new. _____ In

cit - y and in for - est, they smiled like me and you. _____ But

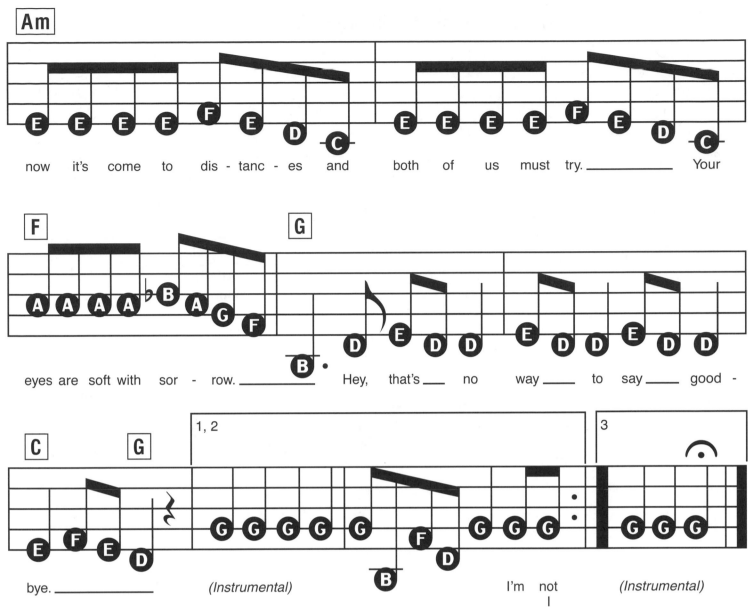

Additional Lyrics

2. I'm not looking for another
As I wander in my time
Walk me to the corner
Our steps will always rhyme
You know my love goes with you
As your love stays with me
It's just the way it changes
Like the shoreline and the sea
But let's not talk of love or chains
And things we can't untie
Your eyes are soft with sorrow
Hey, that's no way to say goodbye

3. I loved you in the morning
Our kisses deep and warm
Your hair upon the pillow
Like a sleepy golden storm
Yes, many loved before us
I know that we are not new
In the city and in forest
They smiled like me and you
But let's not talk of love or chains
And things we can't untie
Your eyes are soft with sorrow
Hey, that's no way to say goodbye

Suzanne

Registration 4
Rhythm: Folk

Words and Music by
Leonard Cohen

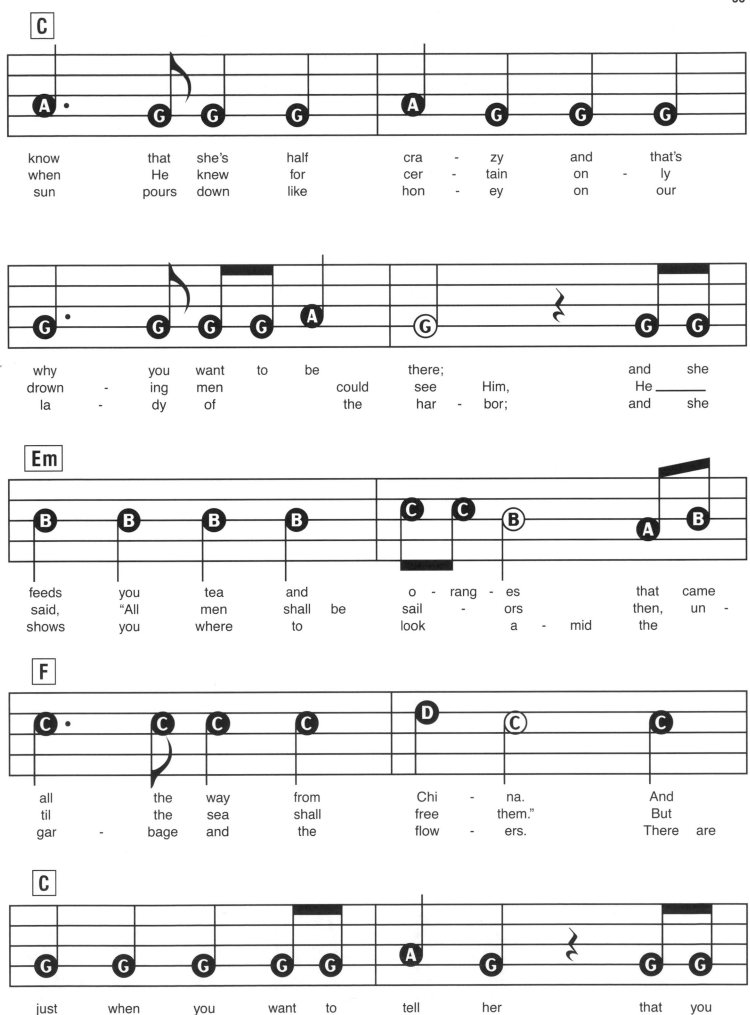

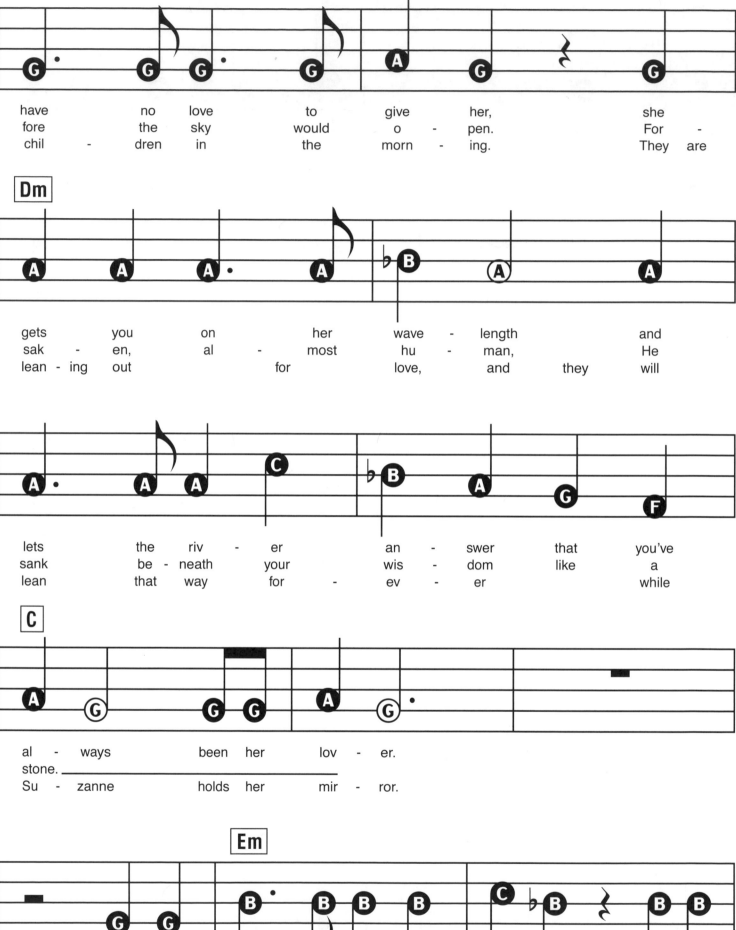

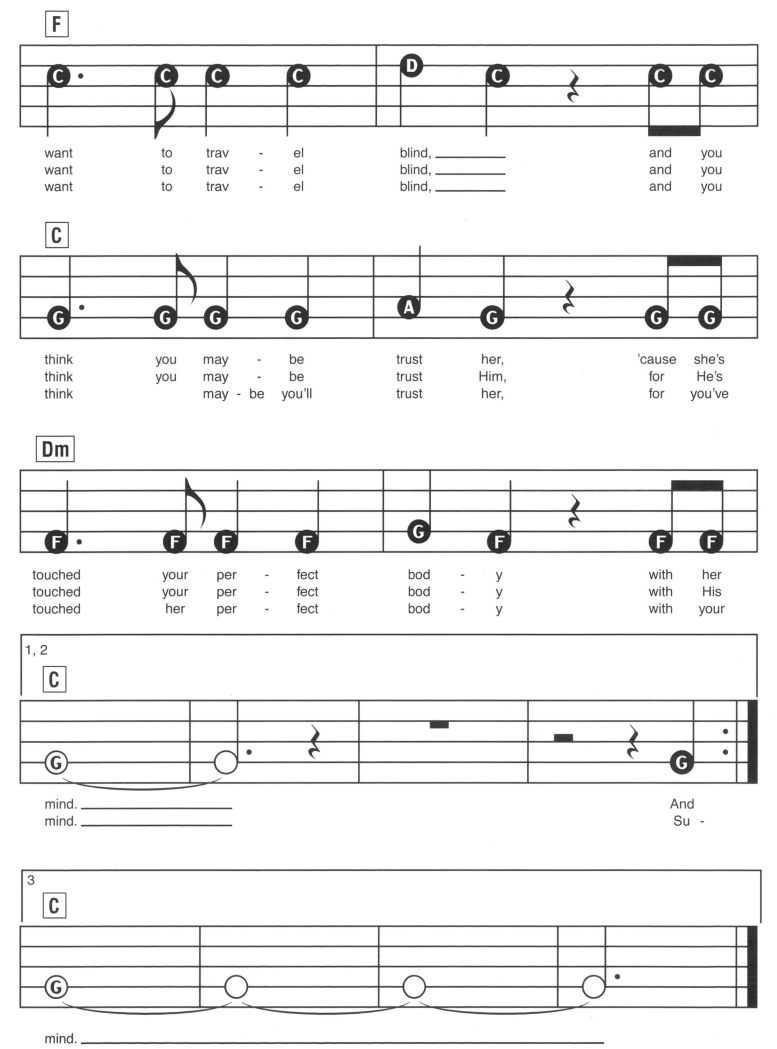

A Thousand Kisses Deep

Registration 8
Rhythm: 8-Beat or Rock

Words and Music by Leonard Cohen
and Sharon Robinson

The pon - ies run, the girls are young, the odds are
tricks, I'm get - ting young, fixed, I'm back on

there to beat. You win a while and then it's
Boog - ie Street. You lose your grip, and then you

done, your lit - tle win - ning streak. And sum - moned
slip in - to the mas - ter - piece. And may - be

now to deal with your in - vin - ci - ble de -
I had miles to drive, and prom - is - es to

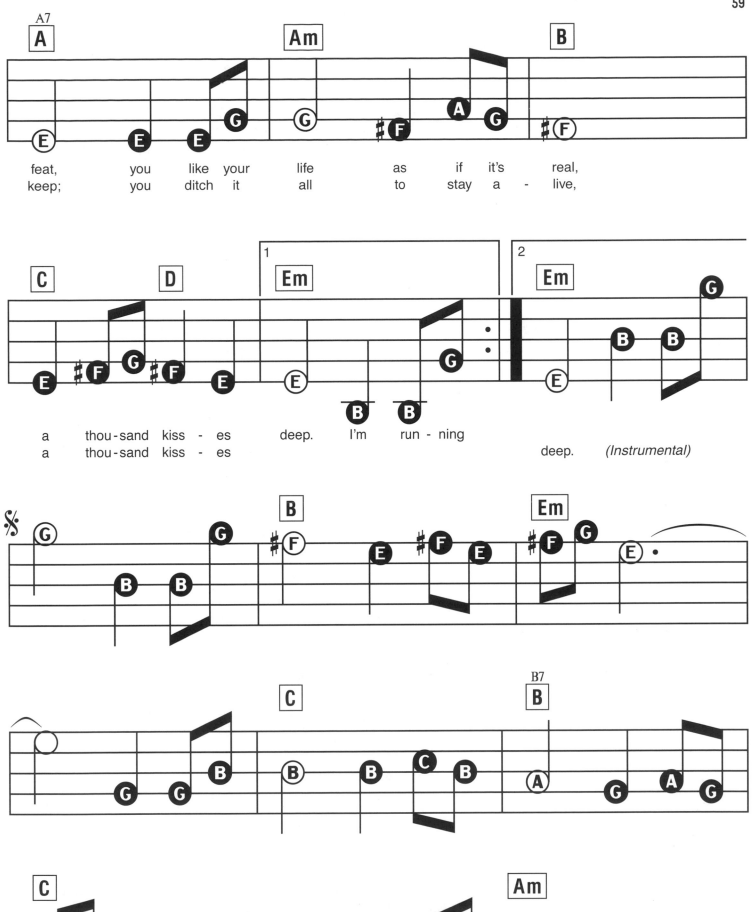

feat,   you   like your   life   as   if   it's   real,
keep;   you   ditch it   all   to   stay a - live,

a   thou-sand kiss - es   deep.   I'm   run - ning
a   thou-sand kiss - es   deep.   *(Instrumental)*

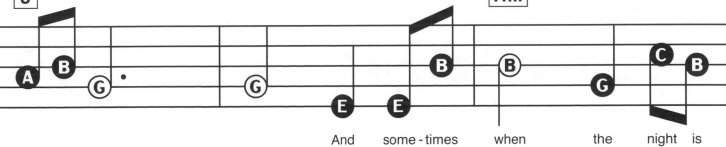

And   some - times   when   the   night   is

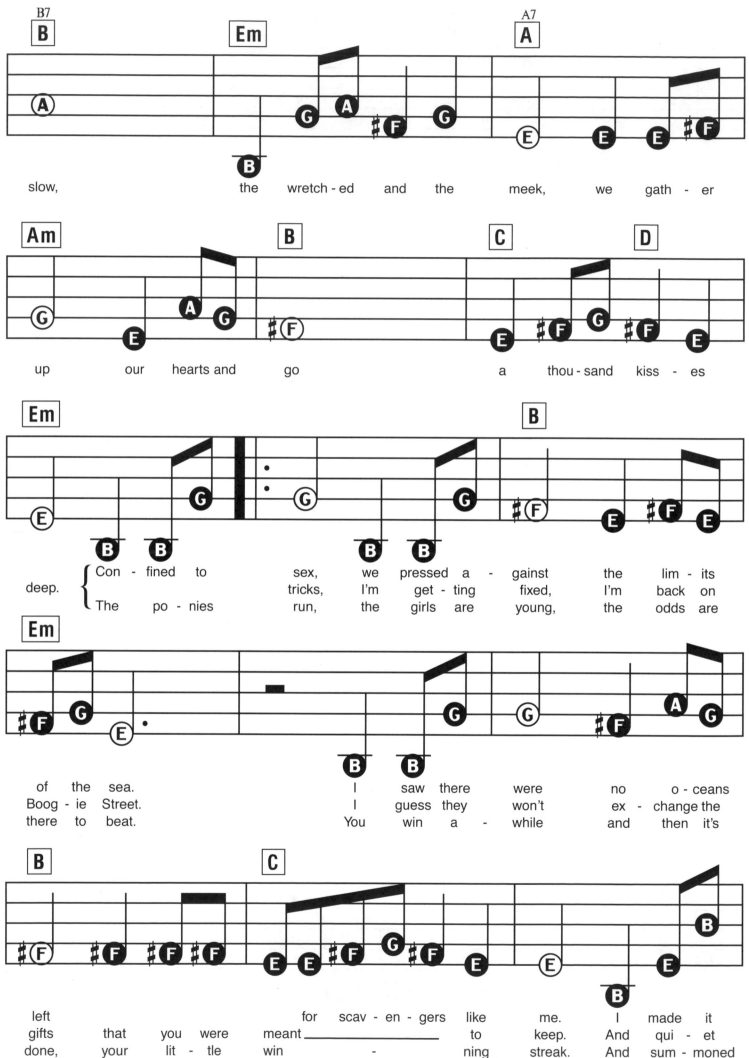

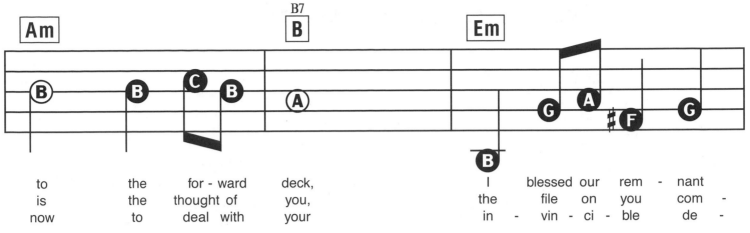

to	the	for - ward	deck,	I	blessed	our	rem -	nant
is	the	thought of	you,	the	file	on	you	com -
now	to	deal with	your	in -	vin -	ci -	ble	de -

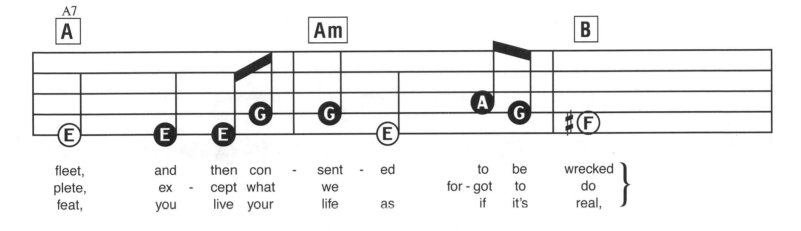

fleet,	and	then con -	sent -	ed	to	be	wrecked
plete,	ex -	cept what	we		for - got	to	do
feat,	you	live your	life	as	if	it's	real,

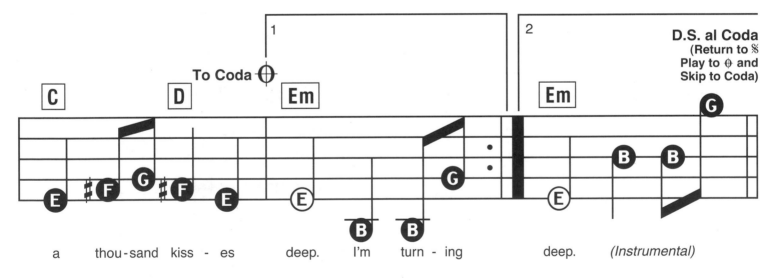

| a | thou - sand | kiss - es | deep. | I'm | turn - ing | deep. *(Instrumental)* |

CODA

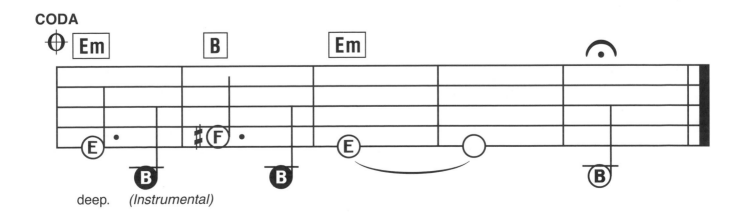

deep. *(Instrumental)*

Waiting for the Miracle

Registration 8
Rhythm: Pop or Rock

Words and Music by Leonard Cohen
and Sharon Robinson

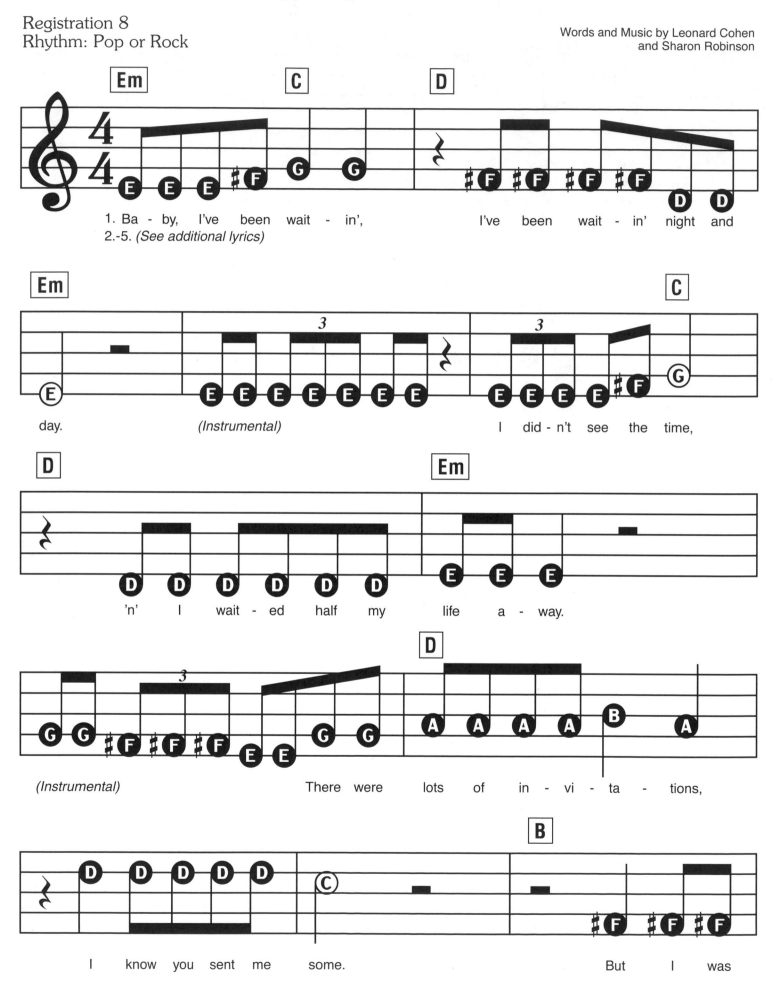

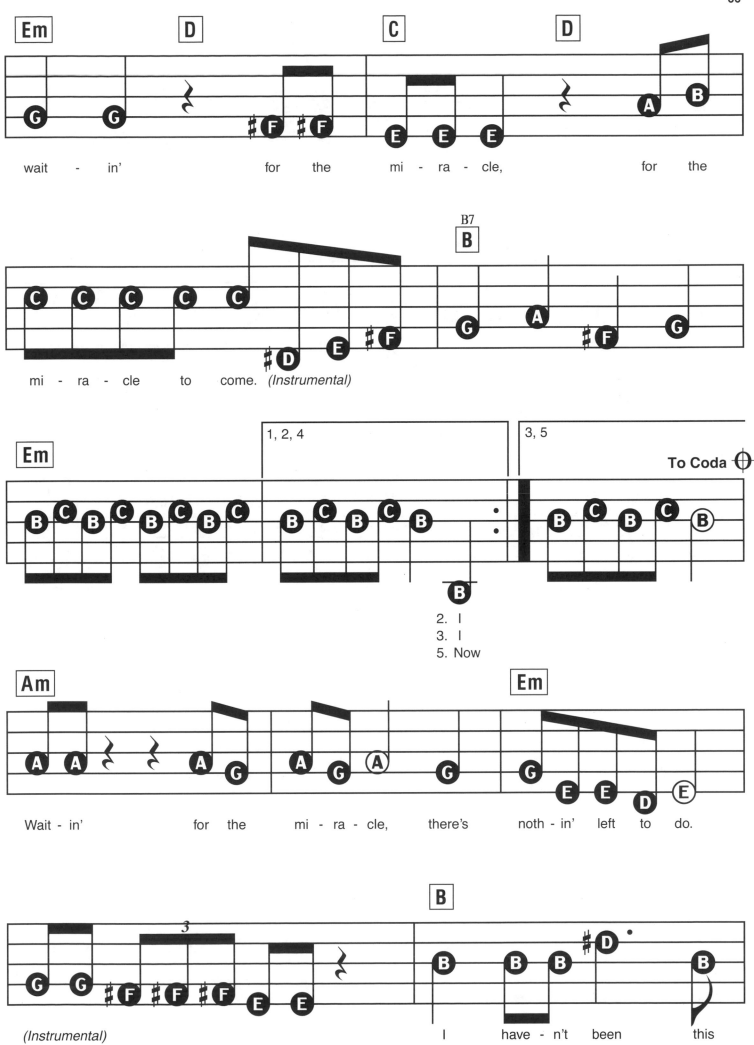

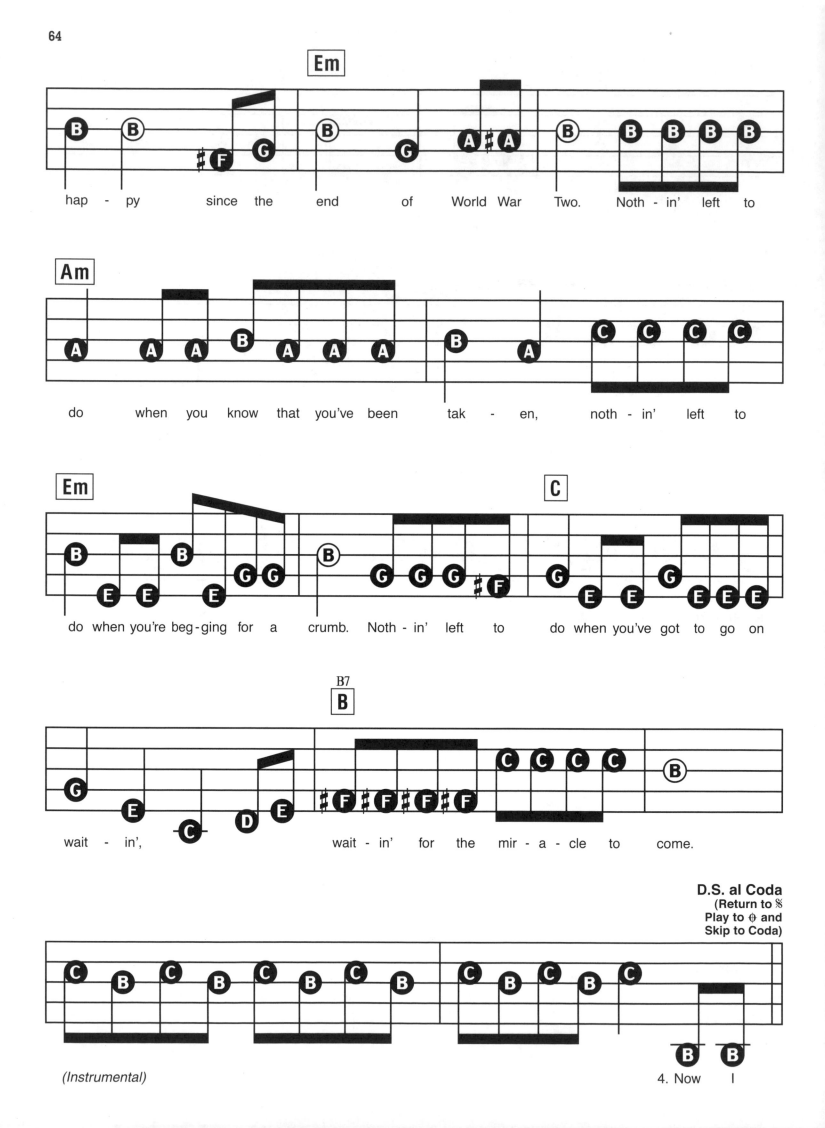

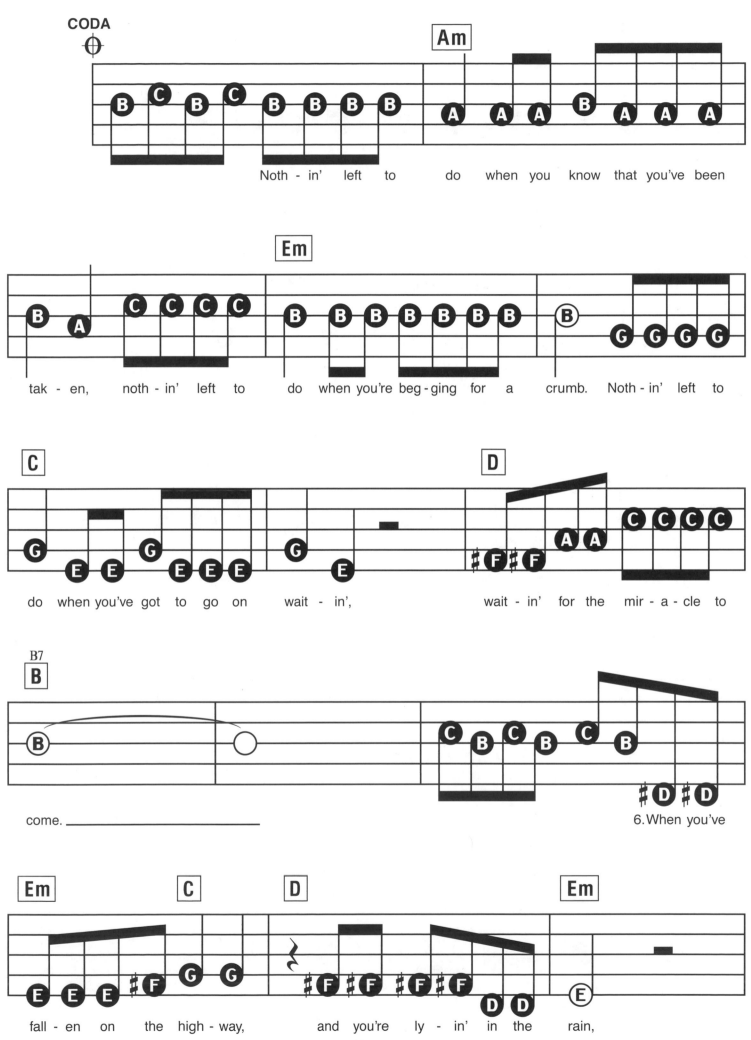

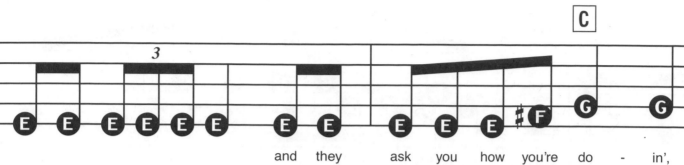

C

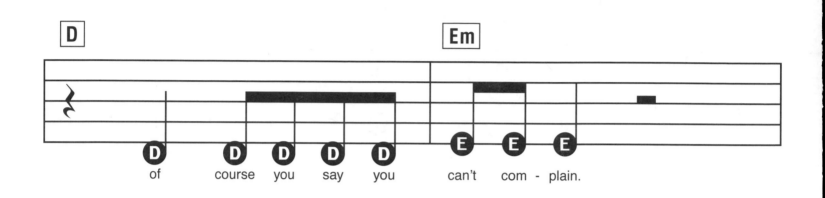

and they ask you how you're do - in',

D   Em

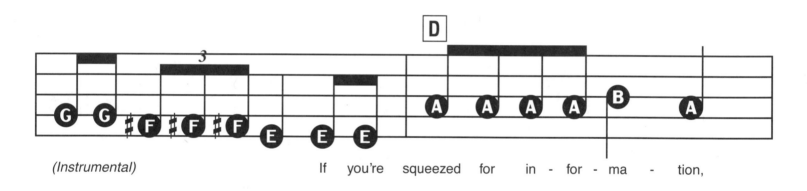

of course you say you can't com - plain.

D

G G ♯F ♯F ♯F E E E   A A A A B   A

(Instrumental)   If you're squeezed for in - for - ma - tion,

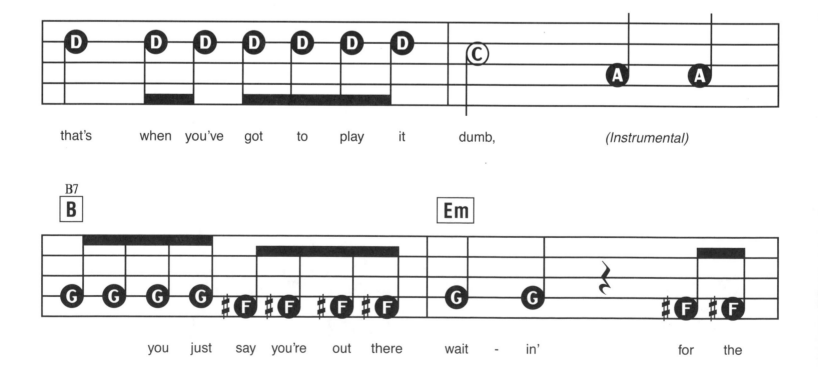

D D D D D D D   C   A   A

that's when you've got to play it dumb,   *(Instrumental)*

B7
B   Em

G G G G ♯F ♯F ♯F ♯F   G   G   ♯F ♯F

you just say you're out there wait - in'   for the

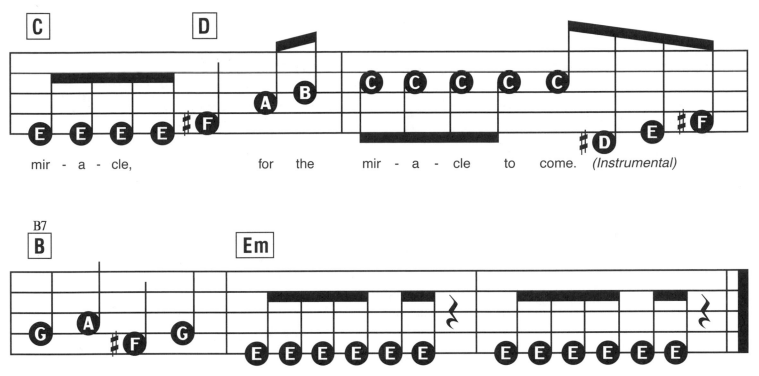

mir - a - cle,   for   the   mir - a - cle to come. *(Instrumental)*

Additional Lyrics

2. I know you really love me,
   But, you see, my hands were tied.
   And I know it must have hurt you,
   It must have hurt your pride
   To have to stand beneath my window
   With your bugle and your drum.
   And me, I'm up there waitin'
   For the miracle, for the miracle to come.

3. I don't believe you'd like it,
   You wouldn't like it here.
   There ain't no entertainment,
   And the judgments are severe.
   The Maestro says it's Mozart,
   But it sounds like bubble gum.
   When your waitin'
   For the miracle, for the miracle to come.

4. Now I dreamed about you, baby,
   It was just the other night.
   Most of you was naked,
   Ah, but some of you was light.
   The sands of time were fallin'
   From your fingers and your thumb,
   And you were waitin'
   For the miracle, for the miracle to come.

5. Now baby, let's get married,
   We've been alone too long.
   Let's be alone together,
   Let's see if we're that strong.
   Yeah, let's do somethin' crazy,
   Somethin' absolutely wrong,
   While we're waitin'
   For the miracle, for the miracle to come.

So Long Marianne

Registration 4
Rhythm: 6/8 March

Words and Music by
Leonard Cohen

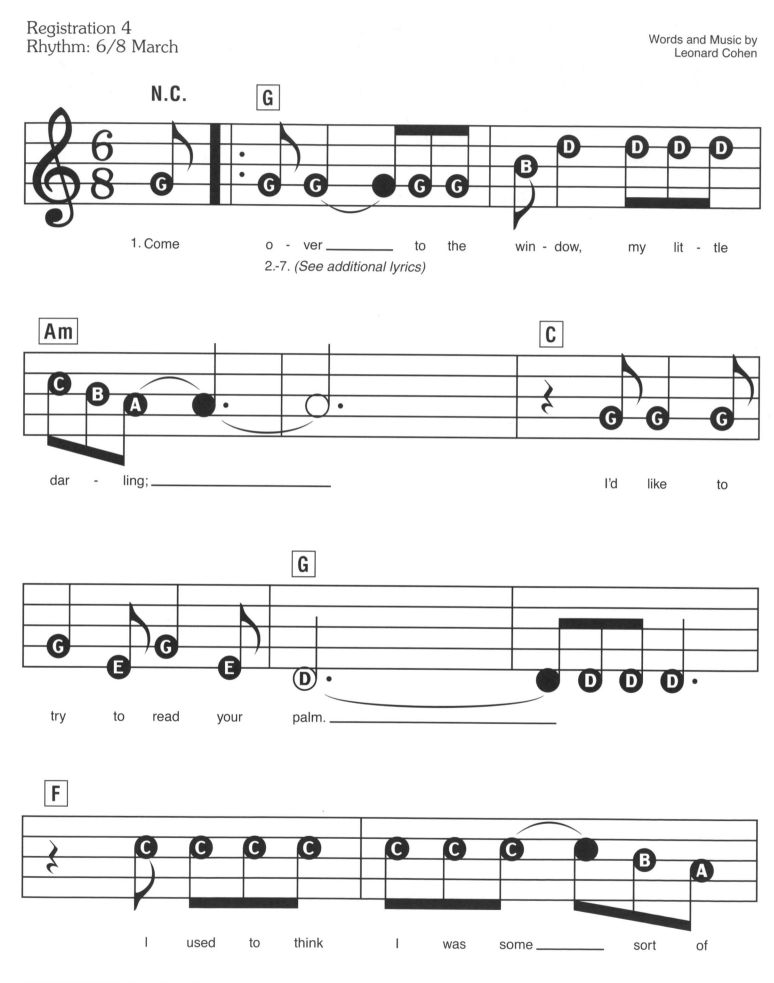

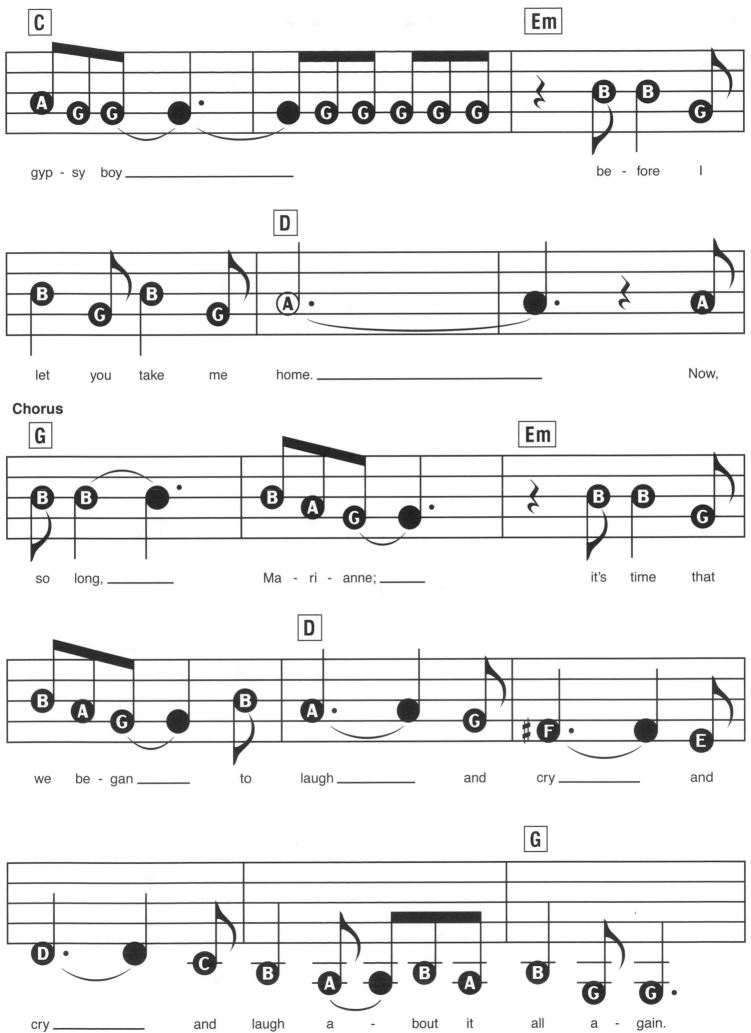

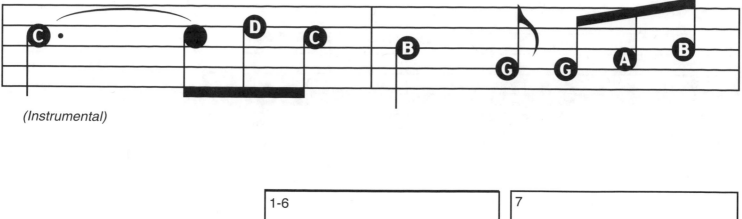

(Instrumental)

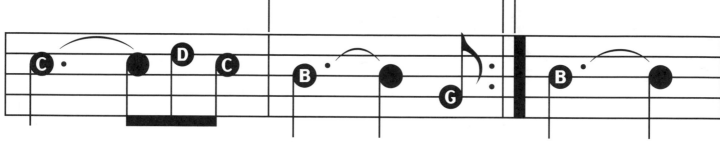

2. Well,

Additional Lyrics

2. Well, you know that I love to live with you
   But you make me forget so very much
   I forget to pray for the angel
   And then the angels forget to pray for us
   Chorus

3. We met when we were almost young
   Deep in the green lilac park
   You held on to me like I was a crucifix
   As we went kneeling through the dark
   Chorus

4. Your letters, they all say that you're beside me now
   Then why do I feel alone?
   I'm standing on a ledge, and your fine spider web
   Is fastening my ankle to a stone.
   Chorus

5. For now I need your hidden love
   I'm cold as a new razor blade
   You left when I told you I was curious
   I never said I was brave
   Chorus

6. Oh, you're really such a pretty one
   I see you've gone and changed your name again
   And just when I climbed this whole mountainside
   To wash my eyelids in the rain
   Chorus

7. O your eyes, well, I forget your eyes
   Your body's at home in every sea
   How come you gave away your news to everyone
   That you said was a secret for me?
   Chorus

Registration Guide

- Match the Registration number on the song to the corresponding numbered category below. Select and activate an instrumental sound available on your instrument.

- Choose an automatic rhythm appropriate to the mood and style of the song. (Consult your Owner's Guide for proper operation of automatic rhythm features.)

- Adjust the tempo and volume controls to comfortable settings.

Registration

1	Mellow	Flutes, Clarinet, Oboe, Flugel Horn, Trombone, French Horn, Organ Flutes
2	Ensemble	Brass Section, Sax Section, Wind Ensemble, Full Organ, Theater Organ
3	Strings	Violin, Viola, Cello, Fiddle, String Ensemble, Pizzicato, Organ Strings
4	Guitars	Acoustic/Electric Guitars, Banjo, Mandolin, Dulcimer, Ukulele, Hawaiian Guitar
5	Mallets	Vibraphone, Marimba, Xylophone, Steel Drums, Bells, Celesta, Chimes
6	Liturgical	Pipe Organ, Hand Bells, Vocal Ensemble, Choir, Organ Flutes
7	Bright	Saxophones, Trumpet, Mute Trumpet, Synth Leads, Jazz/Gospel Organs
8	Piano	Piano, Electric Piano, Honky Tonk Piano, Harpsichord, Clavi
9	Novelty	Melodic Percussion, Wah Trumpet, Synth, Whistle, Kazoo, Perc. Organ
10	Bellows	Accordion, French Accordion, Mussette, Harmonica, Pump Organ, Bagpipes

FOR ORGANS, PIANOS & ELECTRONIC KEYBOARDS

E-Z PLAY® TODAY PUBLICATIONS

The E-Z Play® Today songbook series is the shortest distance between beginning music and playing fun! Check out this list of highlights and visit www.halleonard.com for a complete listing of all volumes and songlists.

HAL•LEONARD®

Prices, contents, and availability subject to change without notice.

1017